Princess Diana

Princess Diana

Joanne Mattern

DK Publishing, Inc.

LONDON, NEW YORK, MUNICH,
MELBOURNE, AND DELHI

Editors : Laura Linn, Elizabeth Hester
Associate Editor : Alisha Niehaus
Editorial Assistant : John Searcy
Publishing Director : Beth Sutinis
Designer : Mark Johnson Davies
Senior Designer : Tai Blanche
Art Director : Dirk Kaufman
Photo Research : Anne Burns Images
Production : Ivor Parker
DTP Designer : Kathy Farias

First American Edition, 2006

06 07 08 09 10 9 8 7 6 5 4 3 2 1
Published in the United States
by DK Publishing, Inc.
375 Hudson Street, New York, New York 10014

DK books are available at special discounts for bulk purchases for
sales promotions, premiums, fund-raising, or educational use.
For details, contact:

DK Publishing Special Markets
375 Hudson Street
New York, NY 10014
SpecialSales@dk.com

Published in Great Britain by Dorling Kindersley Limited.

Library of Congress Cataloging-in-Publication Data

Mattern, Joanne, 1963-
Princess Diana / Joanne Mattern.-- 1st American ed.
p. cm. -- (DK biography)
Includes bibliographical references and index.
ISBN 978-0-7566-1613-7 -- ISBN 978-0-7566-1614-4 (pbk.)
1. Diana, Princess of Wales, 1961---Juvenile literature. 2. Princesses--
Great Britain--Biography--Juvenile literature. I. Title. II. Series.
DA591.A45D5343 2006
941.085'092--dc22

2005026638

Color reproduction by GRB Editrice, Italy
Printed and bound in China by
South China Printing Co., Ltd.

Photography credits:
Front cover/Back cover/Full-title page/Contents page: © Getty Images/
Tim Graham; Half-title page: © Leonard de Selva/Corbis.

Discover more at
www.dk.com

Contents

A Royal Celebration

It was July 29, 1981. For days, joyful, excited crowds had been gathering along the streets of London. Hundreds of British flags hung from balconies and windows. People held posters of the nation's future king and the woman he was about to marry. They sang songs and drank toasts to the happy couple. It seemed that the city was in the middle of a giant party.

The object of the crowd's attention woke early that morning. Lady Diana Spencer had a lot to do. Stylists came to arrange her shoulder-length blonde hair and apply makeup to her fair skin. Designers fluttered around Diana, dressing her in a long ivory gown with a 25-foot (7.6 meter) train. Today was the day of Lady Diana's wedding to the Prince of Wales, and a day of national celebration.

Finally, it was time for Lady Diana and her father, Earl Spencer, to enter a specially designed carriage called the "Glass Coach." Like Cinderella being whisked to the ball, Lady Diana rode to her wedding with the cheers of thousands of people ringing in her ears. After the wedding, thousands more gathered outside the gates of the royal family's home at Buckingham Palace to watch the newlyweds kiss on the balcony.

For months, the world had watched the courtship of Prince Charles, the heir to the British throne, and his bride, Lady Diana Spencer. Diana had become the photographers' darling, with her shy demeanor and traditional English beauty. Her picture adorned thousands of items, from mugs to postage stamps. People all over the world thrilled to this modern-day fairy tale. Along with the thousands of people who lined the streets of London on that late July day, millions more watched the royal wedding on television. It was one of the biggest media events of the 20th century.

Prince Charles and Princess Diana leave St. Paul's Cathedral in London after their wedding ceremony.

chapter 1

Growing Up

Diana Frances Spencer was not a princess when she was born, but she was a member of one of Great Britain's oldest and most important families. The Spencers had been closely allied with the royal family for more than five hundred years. Many members of the family had served as equerries, or aides, to members of the royal family and were considered close family friends.

Diana's parents were Edward John Spencer, known as "Johnnie," who then bore the title Viscount Althorp, and Frances Roche. Johnnie had been an equerry to King George VI. Later, he served the king's daughter, Queen Elizabeth II, as an equerry as well.

Frances's family also had ties to the royal family. Her parents,

Johnnie and Frances Spencer's wedding at Westminster Abbey was one of the biggest social events of 1954.

Lord and Lady Maurice and Ruth Fermoy, were close friends of King George VI and his wife Queen Elizabeth (later known as the Queen Mother). When Johnnie and Frances married in 1954, they were allowed to hold the wedding at Westminster Abbey, and many members of the royal family attended, including Queen Elizabeth II; her husband, Prince Philip; and the Queen Mother.

It did not take long for the Spencers to start a family of their own. Their first two children were daughters. Sarah was born in 1955 and Jane was born in 1957. Although the Spencers loved their daughters, like many wealthy and titled families they very much wanted a son to carry on the family name and responsibilities.

On January 12, 1960, Frances finally gave birth to the son the couple longed for. But their joy was short-lived. Baby John was severely disabled and died just 10 hours after birth. Johnnie and Frances were devastated. Like many members of their social class, the couple was under tremendous pressure to produce a male heir so the Spencer family fortune and title would stay in the immediate family.

Frances gave birth to her fourth child just 18 months after John died. The family was so eager for her to have a boy that they did not even pick out any girls' names. But the baby born to Frances on July 1, 1961, was another girl. It was a week before her parents chose to name her Diana Frances. It wasn't until Diana was three years old that her parents finally got the son they wanted. The Spencers' fifth child, Charles, was born in 1964.

Diana knew her parents loved her, but she always felt unwanted. Even when she was very young, she knew that her parents had been disappointed that she was not a boy. Diana felt she was a nuisance and carried a great deal of guilt over a situation she couldn't control.

Diana and her siblings spent their childhood at Park House, a large estate in Norfolk, England. The house had been given to Diana's maternal grandparents, Maurice and Ruth Fermoy, by King George V, because the Fermoys were good friends of his son, the future King George VI. The house was located on the grounds of the royal family's estate of Sandringham. So, in a sense, Diana and Prince Charles were next-door neighbors. During her childhood, Diana and her siblings occasionally went to Sandringham for lunch or to watch movies with the royal family. However, since she was 13 years younger than Prince Charles, Diana never saw him on these outings.

Diana and the other Spencer children loved Park House. Although it was large and forbidding from the outside, the rooms were cozy and comfortable. The children roamed the kitchens and the schoolroom and played games in the long hallways. Diana's bedroom overlooked acres of open fields filled with grazing cows. Rabbits, foxes, and other woodland creatures played on the sweeping lawns of the estate, and the streams were filled with fish and ducks.

Despite the beautiful surroundings, Diana's childhood was full of unhappiness and turmoil. The oldest Spencer children, Sarah and Jane, were away at boarding school when Diana and Charles were young. Although Diana and Charles were very close to each other, they felt distant from their parents. In the tradition of the time and the social class the Spencers belonged to, most of the day-to-day responsibilities of raising the children fell on nannies, servants, and tutors. Diana's brother later recalled that he never sat down to a meal with his father until he was seven years old.

Much of Diana's unhappiness came from the deteriorating relationship between her parents. The Spencers' marriage had been strained since the death of their first son. In 1969, Frances and Johnnie Spencer divorced, and Johnnie was given full custody of their four children. Soon after the divorce was finalized, Diana's mother married Peter Shand-Kydd.

Diana had many painful memories of the divorce. She sometimes heard her mother crying when the children

Diana and her younger brother, Charles, were very close throughout their childhood and helped each other through many difficult times.

had to return home to their father after weekend visits. She worried about showing favoritism for one parent over another if they gave her new clothes to wear. Diana spent many nights listening to her younger brother cry "I want my mummy!" from his room down the hall but was too afraid of the dark to go and comfort him. Along with the loneliness and guilt that divorce

Diana shares a friendly moment with a Shetland pony.

causes any child, Diana also struggled with feeling different, because divorce was quite uncommon and still considered scandalous during the 1970s.

About the time of the divorce, Diana was sent to Riddlesworth Hall, an all-girls boarding school about an hour away from her home. She had attended a local school when she was very young, but it was common for upper-class families to send their children to boarding schools when they were about eight years old. Although Diana was homesick at first, she quickly fell into the boarding school routine.

Diana got along well with the other girls and the teachers at Riddlesworth. She quickly developed a reputation as a kind girl who especially liked helping the younger children. She often assisted the teachers with their students.

Diana also adored animals. The students were allowed to have pets, and Diana had a guinea pig. She won prizes for taking the best care of her pet. Diana also enjoyed horseback riding—until she fell from a horse and broke her arm. After that, she was no longer comfortable on a horse, and wouldn't be for many years.

Although she was popular and enjoyed the social side of school, Diana was frustrated by her studies. She struggled to learn math and science, and only really enjoyed classes in art and music. It didn't help matters that her younger brother, Charles, was an excellent student who teased Diana about her poor grades. Diana was especially hurt when Charles called her "Brian" after a slow-witted snail in a popular children's TV show called *The Magic Roundabout*.

Despite her academic shortcomings, Diana did shine at athletics. She was tall and agile and played many sports, including tennis, netball, and field hockey. But her favorite sports were swimming and diving. Her abilities in the water provided Diana with an excellent way to get attention and admiration. Her former nanny, Mary Clarke, recalled, "Diana knew she was a very good swimmer and she used to take every opportunity to

NETBALL

Netball is a women's sport similar to basketball, and is very popular in Great Britain and Australia. In netball, the basketball hoops do not have backboards.

show off. She used to love nothing more than when we had crowds of people round the pool. Much against her father's wishes...she'd run to the top of the slide and stand there poised...and shout to everyone, 'Look at me! Look at me!,' knowing that her father wouldn't reprimand her in front of everyone else, and execute this beautiful dive into the pool."

When Diana was 13 years old, her life changed dramatically. On June 9, 1975, her 83-year-old grandfather died of pneumonia. He had been the seventh Earl Spencer, and lived at the ancestral estate of Althorp in Northamptonshire, England. Upon his death, Diana's father became the eighth Earl Spencer and inherited Althorp. Diana and her siblings also received titles. Diana, Jane, and Sarah were now Ladies, and Charles was Viscount Althorp.

Diana's father moved his family to the huge estate of Althorp. Diana and her siblings did not like their new home very much. It was a large, cold place with many spooky

At first, Diana did not like living at Althorp. It was hard to feel at home in such a huge house.

corners and shadows. Diana and Charles were especially sad about leaving the cozy charm of their home at Park House, but eventually Althorp began to feel like home.

Around the same time the family moved to Althorp, Diana also changed schools. She moved from Riddlesworth to another boarding school called West Heath. Diana's older sisters had also attended this school, where they had excelled at academics, athletics, and leadership. Diana felt inadequate by comparison. However, she did find great satisfaction in one area. West Heath girls were required to volunteer in the community. Diana and another girl visited an elderly woman every week, cleaning her house, doing her shopping, and providing companionship. Diana also attended dances and other social events organized for severely disabled teenagers at a nearby hospital. Diana discovered she had a natural talent for getting along with people

Inheritance

In titled families, inheritance is a very complicated affair. When a man with a title, such as earl, viscount, or baron, dies, the title and position immediately pass to his oldest son, along with any money and property in the family name. So when Diana's grandfather died, her father immediately inherited his title, his house and his lands, and all the financial resources and liabilities associated with them. Traditionally, titles can only pass down through sons, so if a titled man had only daughters, his title would pass on to his closest male relative, such as a brother or a cousin. With some exceptions, this practice is still followed by British families today.

who were ill or troubled and achieved a great sense of accomplishment spending time with them.

Perhaps the biggest change in Diana's life came in 1977, when her father remarried. His new wife was Raine, Countess of Dartmouth. The Spencer children were united against their new stepmother, whom they disliked with a passion. They tormented Raine incessantly with practical jokes and rudeness. Diana's sister Jane didn't speak to her stepmother for two years. This made Diana's teenage years especially difficult.

1977 was also the year that Diana met Prince Charles for the first time. Although Diana had been to the royal family's Sandringham estate many times, she had never actually met the prince. Diana's older sister Sarah had been friends with Prince Charles for a time, and the family connection led to Diana's meeting the prince at a hunting party at Althorp in 1977. There was nothing glamorous or romantic about the meeting. Charles later recalled Diana as "a very jolly and amusing and attractive 16-year-old—full of fun." At that time, Prince Charles was 29 years old and one of the world's most eligible bachelors. The newspapers were filled with stories about whom he was dating and speculation about when he would get married.

Soon after meeting Charles, Diana left West Heath. She was 16 years old. Like most girls her age, she had taken exams to see if she was qualified to continue at school or go on to college. Diana failed her exams twice and had to leave school. Her family enrolled her at the Institut Alpin Vidamanette near Gstaad, Switzerland. The Institut was a finishing school where upper-class young ladies learned skills such as cooking, foreign languages, and sports.

Diana despised the school and was no more interested in learning how to cook than she was in learning to do math. It didn't help that everyone was required to speak French in all classes and at official functions. Diana was one of only nine English-speaking girls at the school, and she was terrified of making mistakes when she spoke to anyone. The only part of the school curriculum she enjoyed was skiing.

By April of her first term, Diana had had enough. She told her father he was wasting his money and begged to come home. Finally, Johnnie agreed, and Diana moved in with her mother and stepfather, Peter Shand-Kydd in London. She was ready to start a new life.

Finishing Schools

Many wealthy families used to send their daughters to finishing schools. Here the girls learned how to be society ladies. They mastered such skills as cooking, planning parties, dancing, music, and speaking foreign languages. Although this type of education might sound frivolous, these skills are important to people who live in high society and spend much of their lives entertaining and traveling around the world.

chapter 2

A Popular Teacher

Diana was eager to be on her own in London, but her parents insisted that she was too immature and could not live on her own until she was 18. Instead, she remained with her mother and stepfather and sometimes stayed at the homes of family friends.

Finally, in the summer of 1979, Diana's family bought her an apartment, or "flat" as apartments are called in England. The spacious apartment cost £50,000 (about $100,000) and was located at 60 Coleherne Court in a fashionable and exclusive area of London known as South Kensington. Diana shared the apartment with three friends, Carolyn Bartholomew, Anne Bolton, and Virginia Pitman. The four girls had a lot of fun in the apartment and shared all the day-to-day responsibilities. Diana later looked back on those days as the happiest time of her life. She said, "It was nice being in a flat with the girls. I loved that—it was great. I laughed my head off there. I loved being on my own."

Although the four girls sometimes went to parties or hosted get-togethers at their apartment, Diana was not very interested in a social life. Instead, she preferred to stay

18

home and read or watch television. She especially enjoyed soap operas such as a long-running show called *Coronation Street,* and entertainment programs such as the music countdown show *Top of the Pops.*

Carolyn Bartholomew was Diana's roommate and best friend during their London days.

On weekends, Diana usually went up to Althorp to spend time with her family. However, she loved living in the city and was happy to return to London at the beginning of the week.

Diana's apartment was in this building on Coleherne Court.

Although Diana did not need money—her expenses were paid for by her parents—she did want to find a job. She frequently worked for her sister Sarah and Sarah's friend doing housekeeping, earning a pound (about two dollars) an hour. She also babysat the children of her sisters and their friends, whose ever-growing families provided a steady supply of babies to care for.

Diana enjoyed working with children and was pleased when her sister Jane told her about a teaching assistant's job at the Young England Kindergarten. The school was located in the nearby London neighborhood of Pimlico and was a private preschool that catered to wealthy, upper-class families. Diana began working there as an assistant teacher three afternoons a week.

Diana's gift for working with children was evident from the start. Kay Seth-Smith, the owner of the school, said, "She was very good at getting down to the children's level both physically and mentally. She was quite happy to sit on the floor, have children climbing all over her, sit on the low chairs beside them, and actually talk to them... They responded incredibly well to her." After Seth-Smith received many compliments from parents about the new teacher, she asked Diana to work mornings as well.

> *"She was very good at getting down to the children's level..."*
>
> Kay Seth-Smith, the owner of the school

Because her job at the Young England Kindergarten was only three days a week, Diana signed on with several agencies that provided nannies to families in the area. Her favorite client was Mary Robertson. Diana loved caring for Mary's son Patrick. Diana and Mary became such good friends that Diana later invited Mary to her wedding.

Diana was very happy with her life in London during 1979 and 1980. Her academic inadequacies were no longer important. She had two jobs working with children, which she loved and was very good at. She had a comfortable home she shared with her best friends. Life was full of fun and excitement.

Diana sits with two of her students at the Young England Kindergarten. She was a very popular teacher.

Polo, The Sport of Kings

Polo has been called the "sport of kings." It has been a popular sport for thousands of years. Polo features two opposing teams mounted on horseback. Each team uses mallets to hit a small ball through the other team's goal to score points. A game is divided into periods, called "chukkers." Each chukker is seven minutes long, and games have six to eight periods, depending on what country they are played in.

Although it might seem surprising that an upper-class, titled woman would be working at low-paying jobs, Diana's situation was actually quite common among girls of her social class. Even in 1980, the goal of most aristocratic young ladies was to find a good husband and have children. An education or a high-paying job just weren't important to members of Diana's social class.

Diana and her friends were part of a group called the Sloane Rangers. The name came from Sloane Square, an exclusive neighborhood where many of them lived. Sloane Rangers wore conservative clothes. They spent much of their time going to parties, dinners, and charity balls, which were featured in the pages of high-society magazines. Weekends were spent in the country, and often included hunting excursions or more parties.

The upper-class and aristocratic Sloane Ranger women socialized with wealthy young men who were often bankers,

ARISTOCRATIC

Someone who is aristocratic is part of the ruling class or of the nobility, such as dukes, duchesses, earls, and ladies.

stockbrokers, army officers, or heirs to business fortunes. Diana and her friends dated many of these young men, although Diana never had a serious relationship with any of them. She told her friends she was waiting for "Mr. Right." She hinted that "Mr. Right" might be a member of the royal family. Most of her friends assumed she meant Prince Andrew, the second son of the queen, who was only a year older than Diana. However, Diana had a different prince in mind.

Sloane Square is the area of London where many of Diana's friends lived and socialized.

Growing Up Royal

Prince Charles was born in 1948, and was the first child of Queen Elizabeth II and her husband, Prince Philip. In 1958, when he was 10 years old, his mother gave him the title of Prince of Wales, which is an honorary title that is given to the eldest son of the reigning monarch.

Charles's childhood was privileged, but it was also lonely. He hardly ever saw his parents and spent most of his childhood at boarding schools. A serious, shy boy, he was intensely lonely and unhappy much of the time. Later, Charles served in the Royal Navy and trained as an airplane pilot. He traveled all over the world representing his family and Great Britain. Because of his position, he never had the freedom most young people take for granted. Much of his life has been focused on preparing to be king someday.

In July 1980, Diana's friend Philip de Pass asked her to a weekend party at his home in the country. Among other activities, Diana and Philip went to watch Prince Charles play polo. After the match, Diana had a chance to talk to Charles as they sat together at a barbecue at Philip's house. Diana asked Charles how he was coping with the recent loss of his godfather, Lord Louis Mountbatten, who had been assassinated nine months earlier, in November 1979. Mountbatten had been an important father figure to Charles, and the two had been extremely close.

Charles was shocked. Most people did not bring up sensitive subjects to him, instead talking about safer topics, such as the weather or polo. Charles was thrilled to meet someone who was not afraid to talk about sad events and really seemed to care about his feelings. The two spent much of the evening talking, and Charles decided he wanted to see this lovely and thoughtful woman again. He even invited her to come back to Buckingham Palace with him the next morning, but Diana declined, saying it would be rude to leave her host, Philip de Pass. Still, Diana knew that she and Prince Charles would see each other again.

A few weeks after their conversation at the party, Charles invited Diana to go to a performance of

Polo is Prince Charles's favorite sport.

Verdi's *Requiem*, a symphony being performed at London's Royal Albert Hall. Diana attended with her grandmother, Lady Ruth Fermoy, who served as the couple's chaperone. Afterward, the three of them went back to Buckingham Palace, one of the many homes of the royal family, for a late dinner. More invitations followed. Diana was a guest on the royal yacht *Britannia* during a sailing regatta, or a series of races, known as Cowes Week. Soon afterward, Charles invited Diana to go to the royal estate of Balmoral for the weekend. Balmoral is located in Scotland and the royal family spends a lot of time there duing the summer months.

Diana was terrified to spend the weekend at Balmoral, afraid she would do something wrong and embarrass herself. But she was not about to turn down such an important invitation. She consulted with her sister Jane, whose husband was a member of the royal staff, and prepared to do her best

This is the royal yacht *Britannia*. It is 412 feet, 3 inches long.

under the scrutiny of the royal family. Diana's worries were for nothing. She not only impressed the royal family, but had a lovely time, as well. She enjoyed long walks, fishing trips, and barbecues with Charles and his friends and family.

What Diana didn't count on was the scrutiny of the press. As she and Charles were fishing by the banks of the River Dee one day, Diana saw the glint of a pair of binoculars in the bushes across the river. A reporter and two photographers were hiding there, hoping to find out the identity of Prince Charles's latest girlfriend. Although Diana was able to foil their efforts by wrapping her head in a scarf, it didn't take long for the press to find out who she was. From then on, Diana's life would never be the same.

Diana's secret was out shortly after she returned to London from Balmoral. From then on, she and her friends were under siege. Reporters waited outside their apartment and followed Diana whenever she got into her car. One newspaper photographer even rented the apartment across the street so he could focus his camera on Diana's bedroom. Reporters called the apartment constantly, even in the middle of the night, trying to get an interview or just a confirmation from Diana that she was dating the Prince of Wales. Through it all, Diana remained calm and polite. The public soon came to adore the charming young woman.

The newspapers also discovered where Diana worked and began waiting for her outside the Young England Kindergarten. Diana and her boss, Kay Seth-Smith, agreed that Diana would pose for a photograph. Several children were chosen to appear in the photo with her, and the result was charming. However, the photo showed more than anyone expected. Diana was wearing a sheer skirt that day and was photographed with the sun behind her. The sun shone through the skirt, lighting up her legs and making them clearly visible in the photo. When Diana saw the photo in the newspaper that afternoon, Kay Seth-Smith recalled that she "took one look at it, went bright red, and put her hands up to her face in absolute horror." Prince Charles, however, was quite amused and told Diana, "I knew your legs were good, but I didn't realize they were that spectacular."

By February 1981, the pressure on Diana was unrelenting. She spent a lot of time with Prince Charles, including weekends at various homes owned by the royal family. With each meeting, the

As Diana's relationship with Prince Charles became more well-known, she was besieged by photographers everywhere she went.

> *"I am delighted and frankly amazed that Diana is prepared to take me on,"*
>
> Prince Charles told the press when asked about his engagement to Diana.

public and press became more sure that she was the one who would finally become Prince Charles's wife. Journalist Harry Arnold said, "We urged it along and no one could stop the runaway train."

People within the royal family also felt that Diana was an excellent choice. She was young, beautiful, and charming. She was also English and would be the first British-born bride for an heir to the British throne in nearly three hundred years. Since she had never had a serious boyfriend, there were no scandals or secrets in her past that could put the monarchy in a bad light. Diana was also from a family that had been linked to the royal family for generations. Her grandmother, father, mother, and sister all had experience living and working inside Buckingham Palace. This could be a great help to a woman who would eventually become the queen of England. Finally, Diana was in love with Charles, and Charles seemed to care for her, too. The general feeling among the royal family and court advisors was that Prince Charles could not make a better match.

Finally, on February 6, 1981, Charles invited Diana to Windsor Castle, one of the queen's official residences, and asked her to marry him. She accepted immediately, even after Charles warned her that the pressures of life in the royal family would be tremendous. Diana was blissfully happy. Charles

30

seemed to be happy, too, although he was much more reserved. During a photo shoot after their engagement was announced, a reporter asked Diana and Charles if they were in love. Diana said that she loved the prince, but Charles's response was, "Yes, whatever love means."

Diana and Charles posed for photographers after they announced their engagement.

chapter 3

The Royal Wedding

A few days after the announcement of the royal engagement, Diana flew to Australia with her mother and stepfather, Peter Shand Kydd. The three spent ten days at a friend's house. Diana knew this would be her last chance for peace and quiet, but she missed Charles and was terribly lonely throughout her vacation.

When Diana returned to London, she moved out of her apartment at Coleherne Court forever. Diana settled into a suite of rooms at Buckingham Palace. She spent her days learning royal protocol—how to talk to the public, how to shake hands, how to treat the household servants, even how to wave to the crowd. Diana also spent time at Clarence House, the London home of the Queen Mother. The Queen Mother instructed Diana on proper royal behavior. The Queen Mother is the widow of King

St. Paul's Cathedral in London was built between 1675-1710.

George IV and is the mother of the reigning monarch, Queen Elizabeth II.

Diana also met with fashion designers, who guided her in updating her image from shy teacher's assistant to glamorous princess. The pressure of learning to be royal was overwhelming for Diana. It didn't help that she and Charles had very little time to spend together outside of public appearances. She also found Buckingham Palace to be very quiet and formal—a far cry from the boisterous apartment she had shared with her friends.

Buckingham Palace

Buckingham Palace has been the official London residence of Great Britain's kings and queens since 1837. Most parts of Buckingham Palace are private and include living quarters and offices for the royal family. The palace is also used to host official events and receptions held by the queen. Some areas of the palace are open to visitors at certain times of the year.

At the same time Diana was learning the ropes of her new life, she also had to plan her wedding. Many people were surprised when Diana picked two young and relatively unknown designers, David and Elizabeth Emanuel, to make her wedding dress. Charles and Diana also announced that their wedding would be

33

A coin commemorating the wedding of Charles and Diana.

held in St. Paul's Cathedral, rather than at the more traditional Westminster Abbey. They chose St. Paul's because it held more people and provided a longer route for Diana's journey to the wedding, which would allow more people to catch a glimpse of her as she passed.

As Diana struggled to learn about her new role and plan the biggest day of her life, she was constantly in the public eye. The public adored Diana, and newspapers were filled with stories and photographs of her. During her engagement, the press had given Diana the nickname "Shy Di" to describe the way she often ducked her head and looked down when she was photographed. However, Diana hated this nickname. Once, when someone in a crowd called her "Di," she snapped, "Please don't call me that—I've never been called Di. I really don't like it." However, as the months passed, Diana's image changed from quiet and shy to confident and poised. She had a great sense of humor and always seemed to know what to say when she talked to a member of the public. Still, Diana could not always keep smiling. Occasionally, the stress of planning the wedding and her sense of loneliness within the royal family pushed Diana too far. Just a few days before the wedding, Diana was photographed bursting into tears after watching her fiancé play polo.

What the public did not know was that Diana's tears were caused by jealousy. For many years, Charles had been close to a woman named Camilla Parker Bowles. The two had dated during the early 1970s, and Charles had even asked Camilla to marry him. However, Camilla had married another man. The friendship between Charles and Camilla made Diana jealous and unhappy. She knew that after the polo match, Charles was going to see Camilla to give her a gift. Diana was so upset by this that she told her sisters she was seriously thinking of calling off the wedding. However, everyone knew it was too late for that. The wedding was just a few days away, all the preparations had been made, and the stores were filled with commemorative mugs,

Before the wedding, Charles and Diana appeared on plates, mugs, and many other collector's items.

dishcloths, and other souvenirs. "Bad luck," her sisters told Diana when she confessed her doubts. "Your face is on the tea towels so you're too late to chicken out."

At last, the big day—July 29, 1981—arrived. Diana's rooms in Buckingham Palace faced an open area called The Mall, which on the morning of the wedding, was jammed with crowds of cheering, singing people. The sounds of their excitement filled the room as Diana met with her dress designers, hairdresser Kevin Shanley, and makeup artist Barbara Daly. By the time the designers and stylists finished their work, Diana did indeed look like a fairytale princess.

Diana and her father climbed into the horse-drawn Glass Coach that would carry them through the streets of London. All along the way, they were surrounded by crowds of well-wishers who cheered at the top of their lungs. Diana was filled with nervous excitement by the time the coach stopped in front of St. Paul's Cathedral.

Along with the usual nerves of a bride, Diana was concerned about her father. Earl Spencer would walk Diana down the aisle, but a stroke he had suffered a few years earlier made it difficult for him to walk. Diana focused all her attention on supporting her father as they made their slow journey up St.

Diana's 25-foot long train was one of the most striking features of her elaborate wedding dress.

Paul's long main aisle. She knew her father was bursting with pride and enjoying every minute of this day.

The wedding went smoothly, the only glitch occurring when Diana mixed up Charles's names during the vows and called him "Phillip Charles Arthur George" instead of "Charles Phillip Arthur George." Afterward, the happy couple walked down the aisle, then rode back to Buckingham Palace through the delirious cheers of the crowd. The ceremony and the royal processions were watched by more than 750 million television viewers in more than 70 countries. Diana was now the Princess of Wales and the future queen of England.

The festivities did not end when Diana and Charles reached Buckingham Palace. After going inside for a few minutes, Diana, Charles, the royal family, and the members of the wedding party appeared on the palace balcony. The crowds cheered, then began calling for the couple to kiss. Diana and Charles complied, to the great joy of the crowd.

Finally, the couple went inside and changed out of their wedding finery. Then they drove to a private train that would take them on their honeymoon. The first part of the trip was spent at Broadlands, an estate that had belonged to Charles's godfather Earl Mountbatten. After three days in the country, the royal couple departed for a Mediterranean cruise on the royal yacht *Britannia*.

After the wedding, Charles and Diana appeared with the royal family. The Queen Mother is on the far left and Queen Elizabeth is standing next to her son Prince Charles.

Diana was looking forward to the solitude of her honeymoon. She was also eager to spend time with Charles. However, things did not go quite as she planned. At Broadlands, Charles was more interested in fishing than talking to Diana. Even worse, Charles brought a set of philosophical books along. He expected Diana to read the books and then discuss them with him at dinner. For Diana, who had hated academics and wasn't interested in philosophy, this was a crushing disappointment. Instead of getting to know her husband, Diana spent much of the time sleeping or visiting the servants' quarters, where she enjoyed sharing bowls of ice cream and talking to the staff. It was hardly the romantic honeymoon with her Prince Charming that she had imagined.

4

An Heir to the Throne

After their honeymoon cruise ended, Diana and Charles spent a month at the royal estate of Balmoral in Scotland. Once again, Charles spent hours fishing or hiking through the countryside, leaving Diana to amuse herself. It did not help that almost everyone else at Balmoral was much older than Diana, and she felt there was no one to talk to. When she complained of being bored and asked to return to London, Charles refused, saying that the royal family always spent the late summer and early fall at Balmoral, and she would just have to get used to it.

Diana also faced pressure from the press and the public. She had believed that once the wedding was over, the public would not be so fascinated with her. However, just the opposite was true. It seemed like no one could get enough of the princess. She found herself at the center of attention everywhere she went. Diana could not go out in public without a squad of bodyguards surrounding her while photographers crowded around to take her picture.

Even Prince Charles was surprised at Diana's popularity. The two often appeared in public performing "walkabouts," where they moved through the crowds, shaking hands, receiving gifts, and exchanging greetings with the public. Diana was always much more popular than her husband on these occasions. When Charles walked down one side of the street while Diana took the other in order to greet the well-wishers, the crowd on Charles's side was visibly disappointed. Charles even joked that he needed two wives to cover both sides of the street on walkabouts. Although Charles tried to make light of his wife's popularity, he could not help but be a bit hurt that he was no longer the main attraction. A member of a tour to Wales recalled that a dejected Charles had told him, "They don't want to see me."

Being in the spotlight was difficult, but Diana's new position also had many privileges. Along with meeting the general public, she also met many celebrities and world

Royal Duties

The queen and her family have many duties. The members of the royal family make hundreds of personal appearances every year. Most of these are at official functions or at ceremonies organized by charitable or government organizations. The royal family also tours Great Britain and other countries across the globe to meet world leaders and ordinary citizens and present a positive image of the nation to the world. In 1985, Prince Charles and Princess Diana traveled to the White House to meet President Ronald Reagan.

leaders. It was a dizzying new world for a woman who had been living an ordinary life just a few months earlier.

Diana now lived with Charles in two main homes. Their country home was Highgrove, an estate in the countryside of Gloucestershire, England. The large house is located on 353 acres (143 hectares) of hills, fields, and woods. During the couple's stay there, Charles spent much of his time painting pictures or tending to his garden. It was a quiet place of retreat.

Since the business of the royal family was headquartered in London, Charles and Diana also spent a lot of time there. Their base in London was Kensington Palace. Many members of the royal family have apartments in the palace, which is located near the city's Hyde Park. Charles asked Diana to supervise the redecoration of both Kensington Palace and Highgrove, saying that he admired her taste and trusted her judgment. Due to these

In 1980, Prince Charles purchased Highgrove from a British government official.

Kensington Palace

In 1689, King William III bought what would become Kensington Palace from his secretary of state, the Earl of Nottingham. Many famous members of the royal family have lived at Kensington Palace. Perhaps the most famous was Queen Victoria, who was born and raised in the palace. Today, several members of the royal family have apartments and offices at Kensington Palace. The palace is also home to the Royal Ceremonial Dress Collection, a public museum that includes many examples of ceremonial and courtly dress from the 18th century to today.

renovations, Diana and Charles lived at Buckingham Palace for the first 10 months of their marriage.

Diana much preferred Kensington Palace to Highgrove. She liked being in the middle of the busy city, rather than out in the quiet countryside. While in London, Charles and Diana also spent time at other royal palaces. The royal family had its offices at Buckingham Palace, and Charles spent many workdays there.

The Line of Succession

As soon as Prince William was born, he became the heir to the British throne. By English law, the crown passes down from father to oldest son. If there are no sons, or if all the sons die before their father, then the crown passes to the oldest daughter. Prince Charles is known as the heir apparent because he is the heir to his mother, Queen Elizabeth II. After her death, Charles will immediately become king. Prince William is second in line to the throne, after his father, so he is the heir presumptive.

Diana was keenly aware that one of her most important royal duties was to produce an heir to the throne. Diana loved children very much and was eager to raise a family. So she and Charles were overjoyed to discover during the late summer of 1981 that Diana was pregnant.

Diana had a difficult pregnancy. She was often stricken with morning sickness. Despite this, she carried out many of her public duties.

The constant attention from the press was especially difficult during her pregnancy. Not only did Diana feel miserable, but the press seemed even more interested in her now that she was pregnant. After a group of photographers cornered Diana in a candy shop in December 1981, Queen Elizabeth decided enough was enough. She invited all the newspaper, magazine, and television editors to a special meeting at Buckingham Palace and made it clear that the royal family wanted Diana to be left alone.

The press backed off for a while, but in the end, the queen's intervention did not really change anything.

Besides the pressure of the media attention, Diana had another concern. She wanted to give birth to her baby in a hospital, even though royal babies had usually been born at home. When the time came for her to deliver, she checked into St. Mary's Hospital in London. On June 21, 1982, after a long and difficult labor, Diana gave birth to her first son. She and Charles named him William Arthur Philip Louis. The royal family and the nation rejoiced.

A beaming Charles and Diana leave the hospital with their newborn son, William.

The months following Prince William's birth were some of the happiest in the royal marriage. Diana loved being a mother, and Charles loved being a father. Both had grown up with parents who were absent or distant, and they were determined that their son would have a very different upbringing. For the first two months after Prince William was born, Diana and Charles made very few public appearances. Diana breast-fed William for a while and took care of most of his everyday needs, such as changing his diapers, feeding

Although she put on a happy face for the cameras, William's christening was an unhappy day for Princess Diana.

him, and giving him baths. When William was 10 weeks old, the royal couple hired a nanny to help care for William. However, Diana made it clear that she expected to be the baby's main caregiver.

> **CHRISTENING**
>
> A christening is a church ceremony to formally baptize a child.

By the time William was christened on August 4, 1982, Diana's happiness was beginning to fade. Part of her trouble was caused by post-partum depression, which affects many women after childbirth and can lead to exhaustion, sadness, and violent mood swings. Diana also felt pushed around by the royal family, who did not seem to take her and her desire to be a hands-on mother seriously.

Her feelings came to a head at the christening. Diana later wrote, "At William's christening I was treated like nobody else's business. Nobody asked me when it was suitable for William—11 o'clock couldn't have been worse. Endless pictures [were taken] of the Queen, Queen Mother, Charles, and William. I was excluded totally that day." Once again, Diana felt desperately lonely, unloved, and out of place in a strange new world.

In March 1983, Charles and Diana were scheduled to tour Australia and New Zealand for six weeks. These countries are part of the British Commonwealth, and it was important for members of the royal family to show their support for countries that had once been part of the British Empire.

William was only nine months old when his parents prepared to travel halfway around the world. Royal children never went on foreign tours with their parents. Prince Charles had vivid and painful memories of his parents leaving him for months at a time when he was a child. He felt this was a large part of why his childhood had been so miserable and why his adult relationship with his parents was so stiff and formal. Diana also refused to leave her young son behind, and went to the queen to ask for special permission to bring William along. Much to her surprise, the queen agreed. William became the first royal baby to go on a foreign tour.

The trip to Australia and New Zealand was a tremendous success. Huge crowds gathered to see the royal couple, especially Diana, who was treated like a movie star. One of the couple's aides recalled thousands of people screaming and crowding the streets just to see Diana drive by in an open car. Diana loved the attention and was elated at Charles's obvious pride in her.

Although Diana enjoyed the royal tour, it did not cure the strains in her marriage. Charles was proud of Diana, but he also knew that he and his wife had little in common. He had much more in common with his old friend, Camilla Parker Bowles. When the couple returned to England, Charles began going on foxhunting trips with Camilla. Since Diana did not like to hunt, she was forced to stay home and fume at the situation. The press began reporting a rift in the royal marriage. It looked like the fairy tale romance was coming apart.

FOXHUNTING

Foxhunters ride horses and follow a pack of hounds to track down and shoot a fox.

Diana was greeted by thousands of adoring fans when she and Prince Charles visited Australia in 1983.

chapter 5

Royal Troubles

Diana and Charles were pleased to discover that Diana was pregnant again during the early days of 1984. Although she once again suffered from morning sickness, Diana felt better than she had during her pregnancy with William. She was also pleased that Charles cut back on his public engagements to spend more time with his family. Diana later said that the six weeks before their second child was born were the happiest of their marriage.

The royal family poses for a photo at Prince Harry's christening.

There was just one cloud on the horizon. Charles kept repeating that he wanted a daughter and fully expected the baby to be a girl. However, Diana had seen on an ultrasound, a medical device used to examine internal body structures, that the baby she was carrying was a boy. She didn't tell Charles, preferring to keep the news a secret.

"I live for my sons. I would be lost without them."

Princess Diana

On September 15, 1984, Diana returned to St. Mary's Hospital in London and gave birth to her second son. Charles was clearly disappointed, and the first words out of his mouth were "Oh God, it's a boy." Charles also commented negatively about the baby's red hair, which was a common Spencer trait. Diana was devastated—and angry. The moment marked the end of any love she felt for him. Diana later wrote, "Then suddenly as Harry was born it just went bang, our marriage, the whole thing went down the drain… Something inside me closed off."

The new baby was named Henry Charles Albert David, but he would be called Harry. Despite his disappointment at having a second son, Charles loved the baby very much. He and Harry would develop a warm, close relationship.

After Harry's birth, Diana returned to public life. She had changed considerably from the shy, slightly awkward girl who had first caught Prince Charles's eye. As a princess, Diana had access to the best fashion designers and hair and

The Second Son

Diana's two sons are commonly referred to as "the heir and the spare." England's laws state that the firstborn son (in this case, Prince William) is the heir to the throne. The second son (Prince Harry) acts as a backup to the heir. If Prince William should die or become unable to rule before he has children of his own, Prince Harry would become England's next king.

makeup artists and, as the years passed, Diana became more and more glamorous. Her look frequently changed, especially when it came to her hair. Her once layered, shoulder-length hair was now shorter and sleeker. Diana also wore more makeup to highlight her lovely skin and sparkling eyes.

Diana's relationships with top fashion designers also changed her image. She began to be photographed in more stylish and revealing clothes. Fussy, girlish, old-fashioned dresses gave way to sleek gowns with low-cut necklines. Diana's tall, slim figure made her appearance even more striking. During the 1984 Miss World beauty pageant, one contestant remarked that Diana was "the one we all want to look like. The Princess of Wales is number one."

Diana appeared on the covers of countless magazines. Where once she had usually been seen only in the tabloids and gossip magazines, now she was also featured in fashion

ICON

An icon is an object of devotion—an idolized person or item.

magazines. No longer just a superstar, Diana was becoming a fashion icon.

Diana's image as a beautiful, glamorous princess made her immensely popular all over the world. Whenever her face appeared on a magazine cover, record numbers of copies were sold. It seemed that the public could not get enough of her.

While many people admired or tried to emulate Diana, others were simply curious about her. The public was eager to know everything about her personal life, her marriage, her children, her travels, her clothes, and her feelings.

Diana loved to have fun, and she enjoyed popular music, movies, and culture. One of the best things about her position in society was that it allowed her to meet many celebrities.

During the 1980s, Diana became a fashion star, appearing in many beautiful designer dresses.

A monarchy is a state ruled by royalty, often a king and queen.

Famous musicians and actors were often invited to perform at royal benefits and other occasions. It seemed that whenever Diana met a celebrity, the media was there to take her picture. In 1985, Diana made headlines when she danced with actor John Travolta at a White House ball in Washington, D.C. Diana had studied ballet for many years and was an excellent dancer, and the two of them looked very stylish as they danced around the room. Diana was clearly having the time of her life.

Unfortunately, the newspaper stories about Diana did not always document happy times. Although Diana and Charles did their best to hide the truth, many reporters realized that all was not well in the royal marriage. This was especially true in Great Britain, where tabloid headlines constantly screamed "Royal Marriage on the Rocks" and similar dire predictions. Things would only get worse in the months and years to come.

"Then suddenly as Harry was born it just went bang, our marriage... the whole thing went down the drain."

Princess Diana

As time passed, more and more disturbing rumors began to swirl around Diana and Charles. The press noticed that the royal couple was spending a lot of time apart. Some of these separations were unavoidable because of their demanding schedules. In 1987, for example, Princess Diana carried out about 175 official engagements, while Prince Charles conducted a similar number of public appearances. It was impossible for Charles and Diana to go to every appearance together; in fact, having the two maintain separate schedules allowed the royal family to attend more events.

Princess Diana showed off her dancing skills with actor John Travolta at the White House in 1985.

> *"I just want someone to be there for me, to make me feel safe and secure."*
>
> Princess Diana

In 1987, magazines reported that Prince Charles had spent 38 days at Balmoral Castle in Scotland without his wife or children at his side. Reporters—and the public—clamored for an explanation. Finally, the queen stepped in and told Charles and Diana that they had to spend more time together in public in order to protect the monarchy from scandalous rumors. Charles and Diana agreed that they could not disappoint the British public with the truth about their relationship, and made a point of undertaking more official duties together. The royal rumors died down… for a while.

However, it was true that Charles and Diana were growing apart. Diana was still in her twenties and wanted to have fun with people her own age. Meanwhile, Charles was nearing

40 years old and preferred more solitary, quiet pursuits. Most of his friends were older than Diana, and the princess had little in common with them. At the same time, Charles was not interested in Diana's young, energetic companions.

Charles and Diana each had separate private lives as well. Around the time of Prince Harry's birth, Charles was spending more and more time with his old friend Camilla Parker Bowles. Diana, meanwhile, found a friend in cavalry officer James Hewitt.

Diana met Hewitt in 1986 when he became her personal riding instructor. He was an excellent horseman and polo player. Diana enjoyed spending time with him. Soon their friendship would become a popular subject for the tabloids.

Diana presents the winner's cup to James Hewitt after a polo match.

chapter 6

The Public Diana

Despite the pressures of her failing marriage, Diana kept up her many public appearances. She took a special interest in helping people who were less fortunate. During her school days, Diana had demonstrated a special gift for making emotionally and physically disabled people feel comfortable. That same quality was evident to the many people she met doing her charity work in the late 1980s.

In 1987, Diana agreed to open the first British hospital ward dedicated to AIDS patients. At that time, there were so many misunderstandings about the disease and how it was spread that many people were afraid to go near AIDS patients or even touch them without wearing gloves or other protective gear. Dr. Mike Adler, who was in charge of the new AIDS wing at London's Middlesex Hospital, asked if Diana would

Diana cuddles babies with AIDS during a visit to a hospital. Meeting these children touched Diana very deeply.

shake hands with a patient in an effort to show the public that the disease could not spread through casual contact. Diana agreed. Her advisors suggested that she wear rubber gloves, but Diana refused. The photograph of her shaking hands with an AIDS patient, compassion shining from her eyes, appeared around the world and helped to change the public's perception of the dreaded disease. Dr. Adler said the photo "made a tremendous impact, just a member of the royal family touching someone. It was a colossal impact."

Diana also enjoyed visits to the sick and terminally ill in hospitals and hospices.

The AIDS Epidemic

AIDS stands for Acquired Immune Deficiency Syndrome. The disease is spread by a virus commonly known as HIV. The disease first became known to the public during the early 1980s. AIDS weakens the body's immune system and makes its victims susceptible to many different infections. AIDS is spread through the exchange of certain bodily fluids, but not by touching an infected person's sweat or tears.

Diana shakes hands with an AIDS patient. Her willingness to touch people with AIDS changed public perception of this dreaded disease.

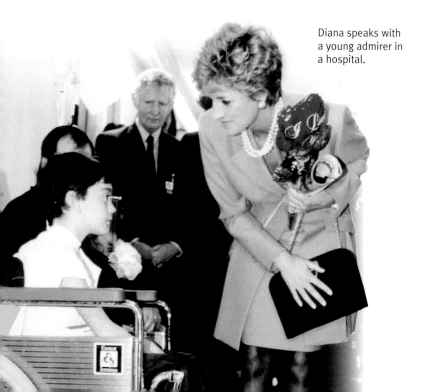

Diana knew that her presence had a positive effect on these patients, and meeting them came to mean more to her than meeting celebrities or government leaders. She later said that she felt deeply at peace while holding patients' hands and talking to them about everyday things, and she was always reluctant to leave.

Diana also had a soft spot for the homeless. In February 1989, Princess Diana arrived in New York City as part of her first solo tour abroad. Her advisors wanted to emphasize the princess's image as a hard-working and caring woman, instead of a celebrity who paraded around in designer clothes. To do this, they arranged tours of AIDS

Diana speaks with a young admirer in a hospital.

> "I think the biggest disease this day and age is that of people feeling unloved."
>
> Princess Diana

wards, hospitals, and homeless shelters.

One of the most publicized stops on Diana's tour was the Henry Street Shelter in New York's Lower East Side.

The shelter's manager, Frances Drayton, was used to celebrities stopping by to get their pictures taken, but she felt that most of them didn't really care about the people or the issues at hand. She expected that Diana would just stop in to meet the directors and members of the city council. However, Diana's representatives made it clear that the princess wanted to meet with clients, especially children. She also asked to spend time with one of the shelter's families.

When Diana arrived, she chatted with the directors, then headed straight for one of the shelter's bedrooms, where she delighted in talking to a little boy about the Michael Jordan poster hanging on his wall. She also talked to the boy's mother and impressed everyone with her compassion and genuine interest in the people behind the statistics. Frances Drayton later told the news media, "The questions she asked, the way she asked them, her concern about not even

CHARITY

A charity is an organization that provides aid for people in need.

asking questions until the press people left, was all out of respect for who we were....Everything was just genuine and she just fit right in....She was happy to be here, you could tell. Such a beautiful person."

Even though Diana preferred charity work, her position demanded that she spend a great deal of time at royal functions, too. She took part in ceremonial events and was seen with the royal family at the annual Ascot horse race in England. Diana also took part in royal tours and other appearances. Her schedule could be exhausting. During one 17-day trip in 1991, for example, Diana attended 25 receptions, 7 lunches, and 19 film premieres, as well as making 108 general visits and walkabouts.

Diana also worked to hide the problems between her and Charles. By now, the couple were living largely separate lives. The young princes, William and Harry, had been sent to boarding schools and only came home on weekends. Diana spent the week at Kensington Palace in London. On most weekends, she and her sons drove up to Highgrove to spend time with Prince Charles. Even at Highgrove, however, Diana spent most of her time with her sons or by herself, not with her husband.

The young princes witnessed many arguments between their parents. Prince William was especially close to his mother, and often handed her tissues and tried to cheer her up after a shouting match with Charles reduced her to tears. However, the public saw none of this. The only family pictures released to the public showed Diana, Charles, and their sons together, looking like a happy family.

Prince Charles and Princess Diana try to look happy for the cameras while attending a parade with their sons.

Separation

As her marriage unraveled, Diana became more and more concerned with her public image. She wanted to be seen as a warm, caring, compassionate person who was interested in social causes, as opposed to Charles, whom she thought cold, distant, and more interested in scholarly and spiritual subjects, as well as horses and polo. Diana felt she had no power within the royal family, so she was especially interested in wielding power where she could—in the press and with the public.

The British press and public were squarely on Diana's side. Newspapers and television stations chronicled her many visits to hospitals and her

Diana's visits with the sick and homeless won her a great deal of praise from the press and the public.

work with AIDS patients, homeless families, and disabled children. It was not hard to find Diana performing these compassionate duties. During the early 1990s, she was the president or patron of more than 29 charities, ranging from the Royal Ballet to the National AIDS Trust. At the same time, Diana began delivering more serious public speeches. She wanted people to see her in a new and positive light.

Charles, on the other hand, suffered from a terrible public image. He was also the patron of many charitable causes, including The Prince's Trust, which held annual rock concerts to raise money to help Britain's at-risk young people. However, he was generally seen as being out of touch with the general public. Most people thought he was more interested in playing polo than holding hands with hospital patients. People could not believe that a man who had been raised among immense wealth and privilege could really understand the needs of the poor or seriously ill. It is ironic that Diana herself came from a very privileged and sheltered background, yet she had the "common touch" that Charles lacked.

Charles's behavior did little to help his image. For years, he had been interested in philosophy and other subjects that struck many people as just plain weird. The public and the press often ridiculed him, especially after he once admitted that he talked to plants. The press also gave him a hard time after he insulted British architects by complaining that the London skyline looked ugly.

On June 3, 1991, an incident occurred that made the British public turn against Charles even more. Prince William, who was not quite eight years old, was accidentally struck in the head with a golf club while playing with friends at his boarding school, Ludgrove. The prince was rushed to nearby Royal Berkshire Hospital, where he was examined to determine how serious his injury was. Diana and Charles arrived just in time to hear that the prince had a fractured skull and needed an operation to repair the damage.

Prince William was transferred by ambulance to the Great Ormond Street Hospital for Sick Children in London. Diana rode with him, while Charles followed in his car. Diana stayed at the hospital during the operation, which was a routine procedure to remove the piece of cracked bone so it would not press on William's brain. Charles, however, left to attend a previously scheduled engagement at the opera. His reasoning was that the operation was not very serious, and Diana had made it clear that she did not want him there. The operation went well, and William was soon released from the hospital to recover at home.

The next day, the tabloids were full of headlines criticizing Prince Charles for his seeming inattention to his son. One British tabloid, the *Sun*, screamed "What Kind of Dad Are You?" Most people agreed with the newspapers, finding it hard to believe that any caring father would leave his son in the hospital during surgery in order to attend the opera. Once again, Charles was put in a position where he had to

Princess Diana and Prince William return home after William's operation to repair his fractured skull.

explain his behavior, while Diana was seen as a loving, caring parent.

The comparisons between Diana and Charles as parents did not end with William's accident. The press clearly favored Diana, and it seemed that every few days there were pictures of Diana with her children, while Charles was noticeably absent. Diana and the princes were photographed shopping, even eating at McDonald's. Diana was determined that her sons would not have the lonely childhood she and Charles had endured, and that they would not be as out of touch with the real world as their father had been. So she sometimes took the boys with her when she did charity work and also allowed them to have normal childhood experiences, such as eating out, going to the park, and playing with friends.

Charles also loved his sons very much and spent time with them, but the activities they shared tended to be out of the public eye. Charles often took the boys riding or hunting on the grounds of the royal estates. However, pictures of him spending time with William and Harry were almost non-existent.

An incident in late 1991 clearly illustrated the press's favoritism for Diana. She and Charles took the boys with them on a tour of Canada. One day during the trip, the royal couple boarded the yacht *Britannia*, where William and Harry were waiting for them. As soon as Diana saw the boys, her face lit up with joy and she ran to embrace them. The photograph of Diana reaching out for her sons became one of the most famous ever taken of her. A few seconds later, Prince Charles was photographed hugging and kissing his sons, but those photos never made the papers. The public was left with the impression that Diana loved her boys, while Charles was indifferent.

Diana's joy is clearly evident as she rushes to embrace her sons.

When Diana turned away from Charles's kiss after a polo match, the world could clearly see problems in the marriage.

Another famous photo showed how relations between Charles and Diana had cooled. In February 1992, the royal couple were in India. After his team won a polo match, Charles went up to Diana, who was awarding the prizes. As Charles leaned forward to kiss her, Diana turned away, receiving a quick kiss on the neck. The moment could not have been less romantic—or more symbolic of the state of their marriage.

Since Diana was so clearly the media's favorite, Charles felt he needed to fight back. His advisors and friends began to talk about Diana's emotional problems. They hinted that any problems in the marriage were caused by Diana's neediness, her constant demands for attention, and her wild mood swings.

Diana was furious and decided she needed to set the record straight. When she heard that writer Andrew Morton was writing her biography, her office contacted Morton and said that Diana would like to help. She allowed Morton to interview her in secret, and asked her friends to speak candidly to the writer. Diana also reviewed the manuscript and wrote notes and descriptions of events for Morton to put in the book. "I was at the end of my tether, I was desperate," she later explained.

When *Diana: Her True Story* was published in 1992, it caused a tremendous sensation. The book painted a vivid picture of Diana as a lonely, unhappy woman who was trapped in a loveless marriage with a man who was cold and distant. Diana also described her lonely childhood and how she constantly felt unwanted by the royal family.

One of the most startling revelations in the book was that Diana suffered from an eating disorder called bulimia. Diana blamed her bulimia on the stresses of royal

The publication of *Diana: Her True Story* rocked the world—and the royal family.

life and the difficult task of pleasing Prince Charles and other members of the royal family. The attention of the media was also a factor, since they held up an impossible ideal of extreme thinness that many celebrities felt they had to follow.

The royal family was horrified when Andrew Morton's book came out. Queen Elizabeth made it clear that Diana had crossed the line. Prince Charles felt betrayed and angry. It wouldn't be long until he told the press his side of the story.

On March 28, 1992, Diana, Charles, and the princes arrived in Lech, Austria, for a skiing holiday. Diana was in a very bad mood, upset and unhappy about her marriage, as well as the public attention created by the publication of Andrew Morton's book.

Diana's emotional state worsened the next day when she received sad news: Her father, Earl Spencer, had passed away. The princess was devastated and burst into tears. Charles tried to comfort her, but she pushed him away. She did not even want Charles to fly home to England with her, even though royal protocol demanded that he do so. It wasn't until the couple's advisors called Queen Elizabeth herself that Diana gave in. Although Charles and Diana flew home together and were met and photographed at the airport, they did not stay together long. Charles went to Highgrove, while Diana went to Althorp to be with her family. Two days later, Diana drove to the funeral, while Charles flew in by helicopter, against his wife's wishes. It was clear to all that Diana wanted nothing to do with her husband or the schemes of the royal family to make the marriage appear

Prince Charles, Princess Diana, Prince William, and Prince Harry at Earl Spencer's funeral.

I miss you dreadfully. Darling Daddy, but will love you forever...

Diana.

stable. A friend of Diana's commented, "He [Charles] only flew home with her for the sake of his public image."

Upon Johnnie Spencer's death, his son Charles became the ninth Earl Spencer. Diana's brother was now in charge of Althorp and everything that went with the estate. He would become a source of support and strength to Diana in the difficult years that followed.

Queen Elizabeth II would refer to 1992 as her "annus horribilis," which is Latin for "horrible year." Her children's marriages were in trouble. That year had seen the separation of Prince Andrew, Duke of York and his wife, Sarah Ferguson, and the divorce of Princess Anne and her husband, Mark Phillips. In addition, in November, a devastating fire at Windsor Castle had destroyed part of the royal palace and its priceless artwork. When the queen asked for public tax money to pay for the 50-million dollar cost of rebuilding, British citizens protested—loudly. They also demanded that members of the royal family start paying taxes on their vast riches. Dissatisfaction with the monarchy was higher than it had been in many years.

The year 1992 also saw the beginning of the end of Charles and Diana's marriage. On November 25, Charles told Diana he wanted a separation. She agreed. From then on, Diana would live at Kensington Palace and Charles would live at Highgrove. On December 3, Diana drove to Ludgrove, the boarding school that William and Harry attended, to break the news to them. She wanted the boys to hear about their parents' separation from her rather than reading it in the newspapers or hearing it from a classmate.

The only thing left was to make the separation official. On December 9, 1992, British Prime Minister John Major announced the royal separation to the 651 members of the House of Commons, one of Great Britain's governing bodies. He said that the couple would not divorce, and that Diana would still be queen when Charles became king. The monarchy would not allow Charles and Diana to divorce, but from this point forward the marriage was over.

The separation came just before the Christmas holidays. For the first time, Diana announced that she would not spend the holidays with the royal family. However, she felt nervous and scared about being on her own. Diana was also saddened by the fact that she would only see her sons for part of the holiday because William and Harry would be splitting their time between her and Charles.

To help Diana through this difficult time, a friend invited her on a skiing trip in Colorado. Diana agreed

and had a wonderful time. Away from the press and the strains of royal life, she was able to have fun. However, Diana was not able to relax completely. She had a lot on her mind. She was struggling with how she would define her new role within the royal family and how she would ensure that she had control over her sons' lives.

"I will fight for my children so they can reach their potential as human beings and in their public duties."

Princess Diana

In 1992, the prime minister announced the separation of Prince Charles and Princess Diana.

chapter 8

A New Image

Diana was pleased to have more freedom from the restrictions of the royal family. However, she was not happy about being separated from her children. Although the boys were at boarding school, they usually came home to visit their parents every weekend. Now, Diana only saw the princes every other weekend. William and Harry spent alternate weekends at Prince Charles's home at Highgrove. The princes also split summer vacations and long holidays, such as the Christmas break, between "Mummy" and "Daddy." On Christmas Eve, 1993, for example, Diana stayed with her sons and the rest of the royal family at the queen's estate, Sandringham. But

Diana takes a sleigh ride with William and Harry during a holiday trip. This was one of the many holidays the boys would split between their parents.

the next morning, she went back to Kensington Palace, leaving her sons behind. Instead of being with her beloved boys, Diana spent

Christmas Day swimming at the palace's pool and eating lunch alone in her apartment. Then she flew to the United States to spend a week with a friend. Diana later recalled, "I cried all the way out and all the way back, I felt so sorry for myself."

Diana also worried that the royal duties would take over the boys' lives. It was very important to her that her sons have wide horizons and experience life beyond the palace walls. To this end, in 1993, Diana wrote a will stating that if she should die, Charles had to share the upbringing of the boys with Diana's mother. She also said that if she and Charles should both die, William and Harry would be raised by her family, not the royal family. The will stated, "I appoint my mother and my brother Earl Spencer to be the guardians." This was a direct slap in the face to Charles and his family. However, Diana's desires would not come true.

Diana might have been separated from Prince Charles, but she was not

HUMANITARIAN

A humanitarian is someone who promotes human welfare and social change to benefit others.

hidden away from the dazzle of public appearances. She still fulfilled her royal duties. During 1993, Diana appeared—and was photographed—at many openings, galas, and celebrity fundraisers. Most of these events were for charity. Diana was committed to doing good works and being a humanitarian. She traveled around the world representing the International Red Cross, spoke at fundraisers, visited shelters for battered women and the homeless, and continued to visit AIDS victims and other terminally ill patients.

One trip that was particularly special for Diana was her meeting with Mother Teresa and the leprosy patients she cared for. Diana was thrilled to meet the Catholic nun, whom she greatly admired for dedicating her life to comforting and caring for the sick and poor.

Diana traveled around the world as a representative of the International Red Cross.

LEPROSY

Leprosy is a disease that attacks the skin, nerves, and muscles. In severe cases, victims can lose the feeling in afflicted parts of the body.

Although the press was always eager to photograph Diana on her humanitarian missions, such as her visit with Mother Teresa, the princess did a great deal of work that the press did not know about. Often, after visiting sick children in the hospital, Diana would go to their parents' homes and ask how they were coping. Diana became close to many of these families and developed friendships

Mother Teresa 1910-1997

Mother Teresa of Calcutta, India, was known around the world for her work with the sick and the poor. In 1952, Mother Teresa opened a hospital for Calcutta's poor and dying. She traveled all over the globe and spoke before the United Nations, stressing the need for people to be kind to everyone. In 1979, she was awarded the Nobel Peace Prize for her work. Mother Teresa died in 1997, less than one week after her friend, Princess Diana.

that lasted for the rest of her life. "I pay attention to people, and I remember them," Diana once said. "Every meeting, every visit, is special."

Although Diana gained a great deal of personal happiness from her humanitarian work, it was also emotionally draining for her. Diana's close friend, Rosa Monckton,

79

recalled how Diana would call her up after a visit and "simply cry, totally drained and exhausted."

In addition to her charity work, Diana also continued making royal appearances and representing Great Britain and the monarchy at official events around the world. In 1993, she became friends with Lynda Chalker, Britain's minister for overseas development. Chalker arranged many foreign visits for Diana.

Diana met many world leaders during her travels. She met the king of Nepal and had tea with the queen of Belgium, among others. British Prime Minister John Major encouraged Diana's tours because she generated enormous goodwill for the royal family and Great Britain. She was still the most popular royal by far.

Although Diana had important friends in Major and Chalker, she still had to follow the royal family's wishes. Sometimes, she wanted to attend an event but was told

Princess Diana serves food to a needy child as part of a Red Cross visit to Africa in 1993.

she could not by advisors to Charles or the queen. In 1993, Diana planned to visit British troops stationed in Bosnia, but the palace refused to give her permission because Charles was planning a similar trip. Diana was also forbidden to attend a memorial service for two children who had been killed in a bomb attack in Northern Ireland. However, the royal family was not able to keep her from showing her support and concern for the people of Northern Ireland later that year. In November, she attended a Remembrance Day service in Enniskillen, Northern Ireland, to commemorate 11 people killed in an IRA bomb attack there. Diana was determined to make a positive contribution to the world, despite any efforts by the palace to prevent her.

Diana felt she was carving out a useful role for herself during 1993. However, a scandal in November of that year rocked her confidence. The owner of a gym in Isleworth, where Diana was a member, took secret and very unflattering pictures

Northern Ireland and the IRA

Since 1922, Ireland has been divided into two countries: the independent Irish Free State (called Ireland) and Northern Ireland, which is part of the United Kingdom Many people in Northern Ireland want the nation to become part of Ireland and have been working to acheive this through peaceful means. However, a small group have used violence to express their anger at British rule. One of the most violent factions is the IRA, or Irish Republican Army. The IRA has been responsible for many bombings and other acts of violence through the years.

of her exercising. The photos were then sold to the British tabloid the *Mirror*, which printed them on the front page.

Diana was embarrassed and angry by this invasion of her privacy. For a long time, she had struggled to keep her private life out of the papers, and this was the last straw. Princess Diana abruptly declared she was retiring from public life. On December 3, 1993, Diana made a speech in which she stated, "I hope you can find it in your hearts to understand and to give me the time and space that has been lacking in recent years." She also said that although she knew when she married Prince Charles that she would be the center of media attention, she had not realized "the extent to which it would affect both my public duties and my personal life in a manner that's been hard to bear."

Diana stated she would make no more royal appearances and would cut back drastically on her charity work. She wanted to spend time in private, reevaluating her life and figuring out what her priorities were without the constant scrutiny of the press.

At the same time Diana was pulling back from the spotlight, Prince Charles was stepping into it. For some time, he had wanted to set the record straight about his negative public image. He felt that Diana and her allies had misrepresented his attitudes and behavior for too long. So Charles's advisors arranged for respected British journalist Jonathan Dimbleby to interview Prince Charles on television. The program was broadcast on June 29, 1994. That evening,

14 million British viewers watched a startlingly candid interview in which Prince Charles talked about how difficult the marriage had been for him. The most surprising part of the program was Prince Charles's admission that he had developed a close relationship with another woman, but only after his marriage had fallen apart. Everyone quickly figured out that the woman to whom Charles referred was Camilla Parker Bowles.

Diana didn't let Charles's television interview get her down; instead she went to a glamorous party.

Although everyone was buzzing about Charles's interview, Diana still managed to steal the spotlight from her husband. On the night the interview was broadcast, Diana was photographed at a party given by the fashion magazine *Vanity Fair*, wearing a stunning, low-cut, bejeweled black dress. The glamorous photo appeared in newspapers around the world, proving once again that Diana was the star of the show.

chapter 9

Difficult Days

Although Diana was still very popular with the public, she found it hard to adjust to life outside the royal family. She felt caught between two worlds: separated from her husband, but not divorced; officially part of the royal family, yet not welcomed by them. Diana needed to find a new role for herself, yet her situation made it impossible for her to do so.

Continued harrassment by photographers and the press made Diana's life difficult during the 1990s.

The attitude of press photographers was especially hard to bear. Their attention had always been overwhelming, but in the past, Diana had had the support of the royal family in dealing with the press. Now, she was on her own. Diana had also dropped the royal police protection, which she had always felt was an invasion of privacy. This made the press photographers even more aggressive.

To make matters worse, a new generation of photographers had come onto the scene. Known as

Paparazzi

"Paparazzi" is the plural form of the Italian word "paparazzo," which means "freelance photographer." The term "paparazzi" was given to a type of photographer who became popular during the 1990s. The paparazzi are infamous for taking photos of celebrities, then selling them to the highest bidder. Paparazzi use telephoto lenses to capture subjects from far away, wait for celebrities outside their homes, and even engage in wild car chases through city streets to get a valuable photograph.

the "paparazzi," their methods were much more forceful and intrusive than the photographers who had taken Diana's picture in the past. Where the older generation of photographers usually kept a respectful distance, the paparazzi thought nothing of pushing their cameras right into the princess's face and shouting at her. They pursued her on the street and followed her car whenever she drove, almost like a gang of stalkers. Diana was caught in a game of cat and mouse, and she did not like it at all. Frequently, she asked the paparazzi to stop, but they refused. The photographers knew very well that they could sell a photo of Princess Diana for thousands of dollars, and that almost every magazine and newspaper in Great Britain was a willing market for their work. And so the cat and mouse game continued.

Diana was also going through a difficult time in her private life. For many years, she had had a close relationship with James Hewitt, a British cavalry officer. Diana felt especially betrayed when Hewitt later published details of their relationship in a book titled *Princess in Love*.

James Hewitt wasn't the only poor choice Diana made when it came to romance. She had dated several men, but Diana was frequently heartbroken when the relationships fell apart after a short time. Her friends began to wonder if Diana would ever find the right man to love—a man whose affections were true and whose feelings would not lead to betrayal and more ridicule from the press.

Tabloids rely on sensational headlines, and often exaggerate stories to draw in readers.

Finally, in September 1995, Diana met a Pakistani heart surgeon named Hasnat Khan, who had performed surgery on a friend's husband. The two became very close, and Diana was soon immersing herself in his world, reading medical journals and learning about Pakistani customs. Khan seemed to truly love Diana for herself, not for her title or her fame. He also insisted that their relationship stay private, so the couple was rarely seen in public and managed to escape the attention of the paparazzi. Diana's friends breathed a sigh of relief. Perhaps the princess had found true love at last.

No matter what else was going on in her life, Diana felt her most important role was to be a good mother to her sons William and Harry. Although she was cut off from most royal functions, Diana still saw her boys every other weekend and had a tremendous influence on their lives.

Diana knew that her sons were leading a privileged, sheltered existence, going to boarding school, living in royal palaces, and having servants to take care of their everyday needs. Diana continued her efforts to help William and Harry see the "real world" where most people lived, and to make them aware of suffering and the need to help.

This was especially true for William, who would be king one day. Diana wanted him to be out in the world, experiencing life and understanding different points of view, not "hidden upstairs with the governess."

To achieve her goal, Diana took her boys on some of her charity visits. William and Harry visited homeless shelters and hospitals. They met and interacted with AIDS patients, homeless families, and disabled children.

Diana also wanted her boys to have fun. She knew that they had their fill of privileged pastimes, such as hunting and fishing, when they were with Prince Charles and the royal family, but she wanted more for them. Unlike most royal children, William and Harry enjoyed the pleasures of amusement parks and trips to ranches in the American West. On trips abroad, Diana and her sons went sightseeing like

Diana, her sons, and a friend enjoy an amusement park ride during a vacation.

Diana won a great deal of public sympathy when she was interviewed on the TV show *Panorama*.

ordinary tourists, rather than visiting national sites and museums privately after hours, as many celebrities did. Diana always looked for ways to teach her boys to understand people whose lives were different than their own.

By 1994, Diana felt increasingly under attack. By keeping silent and out of the public eye, Prince Charles seemed to be winning more respect. His television interview, as well as several biographies of the couple, painted a picture of a stable man who had had to put up with a mentally unstable wife.

During 1995, Diana was approached by a television reporter named Martin Bashir, who wanted to interview her for a British show called *Panorama*. Although most of her friends and advisors were against the idea, Diana believed

"There were three of us in this marriage...."

Princess Diana

that telling her side of the story on TV was the only way to regain public sympathy and put an end to the unfavorable picture painted by Prince Charles and the royal family. The interview was taped secretly on November 5 and broadcast on November 20.

The show created a sensation. It was watched by 23 million people in Great Britain, as well as millions more around the world. Diana talked openly about her emotional struggles and her unhappy marriage. Although she admitted to having a relationship with James Hewitt, she also made it clear that her marriage to Prince Charles could never have succeeded because of his long-term relationship with Camilla Parker Bowles. Diana also expressed her desire to be "the queen of people's hearts," someone who loved others and was loved by them, rather than being an actual queen sitting on the throne.

Camilla Parker Bowles's relationship with Charles put a strain on the royal marriage.

The royal family was furious at this interview. The media and the public, however, took Diana's side. Newspaper headlines called Diana "magnificent" and "brave." It was clear to all that Diana would not continue to be a helpless victim. She was determined to take a stand and make the best of her crumbling world.

Queen Elizabeth hated to have her family's problems played out in the news media, and Diana's performance struck her as nothing more than a spoiled child whining about how badly she had been mistreated and looking for revenge. It was clear to her that Diana and Charles had to stop harassing each other through the press, and that the constant warfare between the two was severely damaging the monarchy's reputation. Although there had been other divorces in the royal family, the queen was very much against divorce. However, it was clear that there was no other solution. Just four weeks after the *Panorama* broadcast, Queen

Queen Elizabeth was concerned about Diana's effect on the royal family and encouraged Charles and Diana to divorce.

Elizabeth wrote to both Charles and Diana and asked them to start divorce proceedings.

A team of lawyers from each side began working through the details of the divorce. Finally, on February 28, 1996, Diana and Charles met face-to-face in the prince's offices at St. James Palace. Diana said she would agree to a divorce, but she had some demands. She wanted to keep her home at Kensington Palace and her offices at St. James Palace. She wanted a one-time, lump-sum payment from Charles's estates; she would have joint custody of the children; and she would continue to be known as "Princess of Wales." Charles did not make any promises, but that didn't stop Diana. Immediately after the meeting, she announced the divorce to the public, along with the news that she would retain her title.

Once again, the queen was furious. She issued a public statement saying that the palace had agreed to no such thing, and that negotiations over the details of the divorce would take more time to work out. Diana was in limbo, her future in the hands of the royal family.

On August 28, 1996, the final divorce decree was issued. Diana received all of her requests except one. Although she was still known as the Princess of Wales, the queen stripped her of the title "Her Royal Highness." Diana was stung, and the public seemed to agree that the loss of this title was simply a mean-spirited act of revenge by Queen Elizabeth. Diana considered fighting to retain her title,

Although Diana cut back on the number of charities she supported, she still made time for many humanitarian visits.

but a conversation with Prince William changed her mind.

"I don't mind what you're called," her 14-year-old son told her. "You're Mummy."

Although Diana was upset by the loss of her royal status, she did not let the public see her feelings. Instead, she emphasized that she was enjoying her freedom and the divorce was allowing her to start a new life. The first step in that new life was to cut the number of charities she supported from more than one hundred to five: the National AIDS Trust, a charity for the homeless called Centrepoint, the Leprosy Mission, the Royal Marsden Cancer Hospital, and the Great Ormond Street Children's Hospital. She also

> ## *"I don't mind what you're called. You're Mummy."*
>
> Prince William

continued as patron of the English National Ballet. She told her friends that she wanted to change her life, cut back on her workload, and focus on the charities that were most important to her.

Public reaction to Diana's decreased charity work was definitely negative. Many people saw the move as cold-hearted or selfish, especially those involved with the many charities she had dropped. Others felt she was having difficulty focusing on her many responsibilities because of the turmoil caused by her divorce. However, Diana stood by her decision and said that it wasn't fair for charities to feel tied to her, since she was no longer "royal," and they would do better finding another royal patron. It was time for Diana to move on.

Diana looks relieved after her divorce from Prince Charles became official.

10

New Beginnings

Even though Diana cut back on her charity work, she was still actively involved in helping others. It wasn't long before she began dedicating her time to a new interest—helping the victims of landmines. The International Red Cross, one of the world's largest humanitarian and relief organizations, had recently become involved in the effort to clear landmines around the world, but was encountering difficulties from governments that did not support the effort. Although Diana had dropped the Red Cross from her list of charities, she was eager to help and called an official named Mike Whitlam for help. Whitlam knew that Diana's

Princess Diana visited Angola to meet people who had lost limbs to landmines.

involvement could generate enormous publicity and good will for the cause, and encouraged her to visit landmine victims and see the devastation for herself. Diana agreed, and a trip to Angola, Africa, was quickly arranged.

In January 1997, Diana traveled to Angola with a British Broadcasting Corporation (BBC) television crew filming a documentary about the landmine issue. She made it clear that this would be a working visit, not a royal engagement, and that she was not representing the British government.

Landmines

Landmines are a deadly reminder of war's devastation. Most countries have used landmines during wartime, including the United States and Great Britain. These mines are designed to lie hidden in the ground, then explode under the pressure of a tank or a person walking over them. When the war ends and the armies go home, the landmines remain behind. It is estimated that there are still 110 million landmines lodged in 64 countries around the world. More than one million people have been killed or maimed by them since 1975. Landmines are especially dangerous to children. Many landmines are brightly colored, so children sometimes pick them up, thinking they have found a toy. Today, many organizations are working to clear landmines.

There would be no dinners with officials and no fund-raising events. Diana was just there to observe and learn. And that's exactly what she did. Diana read up on the issues and statistics during the long flight to Angola. She insisted on visiting a city called Cuito, which was the most heavily mined town in Africa and considered to be too dangerous for visitors. But Diana went anyway. She walked carefully through a minefield dressed in protective body armor, then visited a poorly equipped hospital filled with victims of landmine violence. Later, she detonated a landmine by remote control.

Diana's visit helped bring publicity to an important issue without getting politics involved. Her mere presence made people pay attention. As Mike Whitlam stated, "I can't think of anybody now who could give such a very simple, global message, and get people to listen and take notice."

British Prime Minister Tony Blair and his wife, Cherie, were close friends of Diana's.

Diana returned from her Angola trip with a new sense of purpose. She had long desired a role as a peacemaker and humanitarian, and her work in Africa made this desire even stronger.

Fortunately for Diana, new leadership in the British government was supportive of her humanitarian work. In May 1997, the Labour Party swept the Conservative Party out of office, and Tony Blair became the new prime minister.

Diana and Blair got along very well. Soon after the election, they discussed her desire to take some sort of role as a humanitarian ambassador for Britain. Blair promised to find something for Diana.

Diana's interest in landmines also provided her with an important connection to government officials in other countries. In June, she flew to Washington, D.C., to take part in the American Red Cross's anti-landmine campaign. Diana gave a press conference with Elizabeth Dole, president of the American Red Cross and wife of U.S. Senator Bob Dole. She also met with first lady Hillary Rodham Clinton about the devastation caused by landmines and the need for the United States to support the cause of landmine renewal.

Diana was energized by her work and felt that a new and fulfilling role as a humanitarian ambassador was definitely within her grasp. Her life was taking a positive turn professionally, and in other areas as well.

For many years, relations between Diana and Charles had been very difficult. However, things began to change after the divorce. Freed of their ties to each other and the responsibilities that they had been unable to fulfill, the two were discovering that they could spend time together without fighting. Charles often dropped by Diana's apartment in Kensington Palace for tea when he was in the city on business.

Charles and Diana were also able to present a united front for their children. The two attended many events together, including William's confirmation and a sports day at Harry's school. On both occasions, Charles and Diana appeared comfortable together, smiling and acting friendly. Charles even asked Diana to accompany him and Prince William on a trip to Hong Kong. Both she and Charles seemed to realize that they would always be tied together by their sons and their shared experiences. After the divorce, there was very little of the public fighting and rival newspaper reports that had upset

The royal family celebrated William's confirmation together. William's godparents are in the back row.

everyone in previous years. It seemed that Diana had finally found her place in the royal world.

By 1997, Prince William had become one of Diana's most trusted advisors. Although he was not yet 15, he was mature and wise beyond his years and seemed instinctively to know what would be the best thing for his mother to do.

William knew that Diana was trying to simplify her life and change her image. He suggested that she auction off many of the glamorous dresses she had accumulated over the years, and donate the money to charity. Diana thought the idea was brilliant, and arranged for the respected auction house Christie's to handle the sale.

On June 25, 1997, seventy-nine of Diana's gowns went up for auction at Christie's in New York City. It was one of the greatest social events of the year, and was featured in all the major newspapers and many magazines. Some bidders were collectors, eager to own a piece of Diana's fashion legacy.

Diana previews her dresses before they go up for auction at Christie's.

Others were ordinary people who admired Diana and loved the idea of owning an item from her wardrobe. The highlight of the auction was the blue velvet dress Diana wore the night she danced with John Travolta at the White House. The gown sold for $222,500. In total, the auction raised $3.26 million, to be split between several charities. The event was one of the highlights of Diana's life.

Christie's

Christie's is one of the most famous auction houses in the world. Its beginnings date back more than two hundred years, to 1766. That year, a London businessman named James Christie began selling paintings and other valuables. He was so well respected that Great Britain's wealthiest families began asking Christie to auction their belongings as well. His company conducted some of the greatest auctions of the 18th and 19th centuries. Later, Christie opened an auction house in New York City.

Diana returned to London after the dress auction, only to face a romantic crisis. Her boyfriend, Dr. Hasnat Khan, was having serious doubts about their relationship. Khan was an intensely private man, and he became annoyed when Diana leaked reports about their relationship to the press. He also was in no hurry to get married, despite Diana's hints that she wanted to make the romance official.

By July 1997, Diana was growing tired of Khan's anger and mistrust. She had received an invitation to vacation in the tropical paradise of St. Tropez at an estate belonging to businessman Mohamed Al Fayed. Al Fayed had been born in Egypt and had become a successful businessman in Great Britain. He was the owner of the world-famous Harrods department store in London. Al Fayed's plan was to introduce Diana to his handsome, unmarried, 41-year-old son, Emad, better known as Dodi.

Diana was eager for a private vacation, as long as she could bring her sons. On July 11, the three arrived in Nice, France, where they boarded Al Fayed's yacht, the *Jonikal*, for the trip to St. Tropez.

Diana and the boys had a wonderful time on the yacht and at Al Fayed's estate. They went snorkeling and swimming off Al Fayed's private beach and enjoyed sumptuous meals prepared by his personal chefs. Diana enjoyed Dodi Fayed's

Harrods

Harrods has been Great Britain's premier department store for more than one-hundred years. The store is located in the fashionable London neighborhood of Knightsbridge and was founded by Charles Henry Harrod in 1849. By the 1890s, the store offered a wide range of products, from food to furniture. By 1902, Harrods was London's biggest and most luxurious store, promising "Everything for Everybody Everywhere." In 1985, it was purchased by Mohamed Al Fayed, who undertook a massive rebuilding project to ensure the store remained luxurious and fashionable. Today, Harrods is not only a place to shop, but one of London's most popular tourist attractions.

(he had dropped the "Al" from his name) company as well, and the two spent many hours talking together on the beach. They shared similar backgrounds—privileged but lonely childhoods with distant parents—and Diana was charmed by Dodi's warm, generous personality.

Dodi had a reputation for being a ladies' man, and newspapers were soon trumpeting the pair's romance and calling them "The Princess and the Playboy." Diana didn't care. She was having a marvelous time.

Diana and Harry enjoy a moment together on the *Jonikal*.

11

Diana's Last Day

Diana returned from her vacation feeling refreshed and energized. She couldn't wait to see Dodi again. However, first she had to attend a sad event: the funeral of her friend, fashion designer Gianni Versace, who had been murdered in Florida. On July 22, Diana traveled to Milan, Italy, for the service attended by celebrities from the worlds of fashion, music, and movies.

No sooner had Diana returned from Milan than Dodi invited her to Paris for a romantic weekend. Diana returned to London briefly to send her sons off for their annual six-week holiday at Balmoral with their father, then she rejoined Dodi on the *Jonikal*. Although the pair had known each other for less than two weeks, their connection was very close. They spent as much time as they could together over the next month, while newspapers and tabloids breathlessly reported the new romance. Diana told a friend she had never been happier.

On August 30, Diana and Dodi arrived in Paris after another Mediterranean cruise on the *Jonikal*. The visit would be a short one, as Diana planned to return to London the next day to see her sons after their holiday at Balmoral. She was looking forward to spending a few days with the boys before they went back to school.

Dodi and Diana arrived in Paris during the afternoon. Dodi's driver, Henri Paul, got them safely to a hotel called the Ritz, despite being chased by a pack of paparazzi on motorcycles who nearly caused the car to crash.

Diana and Dodi had intended to eat dinner at a restaurant outside of the hotel, but the press attention was so intense that they decided to return to the Ritz. About 20 photographers lined the walkway in front of the Ritz, snapping pictures of the couple as they passed. Although Dodi seemed upset and stressed by the attention, Diana smiled as she made her way into the hotel. They ordered a meal at the hotel's restaurant, but once again, the paparazzi seemed too close. Around 10:00 pm, Diana and Dodi disappeared upstairs to have their dinner in a private suite, away from the public's prying eyes.

The Ritz is one of the fanciest hotels in Paris. Diana and Dodi Fayed had their last dinner there on August 30, 1997.

Hotel security cameras show Princess Diana and Dodi Fayed entering the Ritz.

After dinner, Dodi and Diana decided to leave the hotel by the back entrance, in hopes of eluding the paparazzi. Accompanying them were Henri Paul, the driver, and Dodi's bodyguard, Trevor Rees-Jones. Paul, who many people considered to be an alcoholic, had been drinking that night and had also taken several medications. Earlier that night, Paul had taunted the paparazzi outside the hotel, saying they would never catch Dodi and Diana.

Paul pulled up to the back entrance in a Mercedes, and Rees-Jones, Diana, and Dodi quickly got inside. The car pulled away at 12:20 am on the morning of August 31.

Despite these efforts, a group of photographers figured out what was going on and was waiting at the Ritz's back entrance. As soon as the Mercedes pulled away, they followed. By the time Dodi's car pulled onto the street, at least six cars and motorcycles were in hot pursuit.

Paul ran a red light and zoomed onto the Place de la Concorde, one of Paris's most famous streets. Paul zigzagged

through traffic, picking up speed as he headed toward the Seine River and onto a street called the Cours la Reine. Eyewitnesses estimated the car was traveling more than one hundred miles per hour, well over Paris's speed limit of 30 miles per hour. Despite the high speeds, only Rees-Jones was wearing a seat belt.

Paul drove into the Alma Tunnel, which crosses under the Seine. The car was traveling so fast that when it hit a dip at the entrance, it almost became airborne. As Paul struggled to control the car, he saw a small, white car in front of him. Paul swerved wildly to avoid hitting it. But it was too late to avoid a terrible tragedy.

The Mercedes clipped the white car, breaking its taillight, as well as the headlight on the Mercedes. The Mercedes brushed against one of the tunnel's columns, then plowed straight into another column with a deafening crash. The impact spun the car around before it slammed into the wall.

The crash was devastating. The front of the car was completely smashed in, although the back was not badly damaged. Henri Paul and Dodi Fayed were killed instantly by massive injuries to their chests, legs, and heads. Trevor Rees-Jones, the only person wearing a seat belt, survived, but had severe head and facial injuries.

Diana was also badly injured, but still alive. She lay on the floor between the front and back seats, unconscious.

Diana's death was front-page news around the world. Millions of people awoke to the shocking news.

As eyewitnesses called the police, the paparazzi caught

> *"The camera flashes were going off like machine gun fire."*
>
> A witness's description of the scene of the accident

up to the crash and began taking pictures of the mangled car and its occupants. An American tourist described the scene: "Photographers were swarming all over the car, snapping as many photos as they could." A policeman at the scene added, "The camera flashes were going off like machine gun fire."

Meanwhile, an emergency room physician named Frédéric Mailliez happened upon the scene on his way home from a party. He did his best to help Diana before the ambulance arrived.

Six minutes after the accident, the first ambulance arrived. French ambulances are like traveling emergency rooms, and Diana was treated at the scene for 45 minutes rather than rushed to the hospital immediately. During that time, the paramedics desperately tried to stabilize her breathing and her blood pressure. Although Diana did not seem to be badly injured, she was losing a lot of blood internally. The situation was very grave.

Diana was taken to the Pitié-Salpêtrière hospital on the opposite side of the Seine. Although it was not the closest hospital to the scene, it was the best equipped to handle severe emergencies. It was just after 2:00 am when the ambulance pulled in, and by then Diana had already gone into cardiac arrest. Diana was carried into

> *"She was the people's princess, and that's how she will stay, how she will remain—in our hearts and in our memories forever."*

British Prime minister Tony Blair's response
to the death of Princess Diana

the operating room, where it was discovered that she was bleeding internally. Although the doctors tried desperately to save her, Princess Diana died at about 4:00 AM on August 31, 1997.

As doctors worked to save Diana, a call had gone out to the British ambassador in France, who in turn called the royal family at Balmoral. Prince Charles was shocked to learn that Diana had been seriously injured. According to press reports, he told the queen, but both agreed not to wake William and Harry to tell them yet.

When word came of Diana's death, Prince Charles's obvious grief surprised everyone who saw him. According to royal aides, Charles cried out, then burst into uncontrollable tears. Queen Elizabeth, who was not a demonstrative person, remained calm and cool when she heard the news.

Following the death of Princess Diana, a memorial of flowers and cards was created above the Alma Tunnel.

Soon after Diana's death, word reached the media around the world. Although Diana's accident had been reported, early information indicated that she had not been seriously injured, so news of her death came as a complete shock to many people who had only heard the early reports before going to bed. As world leaders hurried to express their sorrow, British Prime Minister Tony Blair summed up what was about to happen: "This is going to produce real public grief on a scale that is hard to imagine."

chapter 12

The World Mourns

Tony Blair was right. People all over the world reacted to Diana's death with a tremendous show of emotion. The walls outside Diana's home, Kensington Palace, were soon surrounded with flowers, stuffed animals, candles, and other tokens of remembrance. Similar displays occurred outside Buckingham Palace and other royal sites, until it seemed that all of London was awash in a sea of flowers.

As the public expressed its grief, preparations were made to return Diana's body to London. Her sisters, Sarah and Jane, prepared to go to Paris and escort the body home. Prince Charles announced that he would also make the trip, but the queen reportedly said that such an action would be inappropriate. Charles usually bowed to his mother's wishes, but this time he refused. He told his mother that the public would never forgive the royal family if none of its members escorted Diana. Finally and

After Diana's death, the area outside Kensington Palace was covered with flowers and other tributes from a grieving public.

An honor guard looks on as Diana's body is removed from the hospital to be flown home to England.

reluctantly, the queen agreed. It was only the first example of how out of touch she was with the public's feelings toward their princess.

The queen was determined that life would go on as normally as possible. Although many people expected the family to return to London, they stayed behind Balmoral's walls, where the queen felt the family could best comfort William and Harry and shield them from the press. Public discontent grew even stronger when the royal family made only a brief statement regarding Diana's death, and wasn't flying Buckingham Palace's flag at half-mast as a sign of official mourning. Even Prince William, who was 15 years old, asked his father why the family wasn't in London and why the flag wasn't at half-mast.

It soon became clear how badly the queen had misjudged how much the world was mourning Princess Diana and how angry they were at the royal family's apparent indifference. Anthony Barrett, an expert on Britain's constitution, announced, "The monarchy must bow its head, or it will be broken." Newspaper headlines blared, "Where Is Our Queen? Where Is Her Flag?" and "Show Us You Care." Finally, on Thursday, September 4, four days after Diana's death, the royal family arrived at Buckingham Palace. The next afternoon, the queen spoke to the nation, paying a stiff tribute to her daughter-in-law.

On July 29, 1981, Londoners had lined the street to rejoice in the wedding that turned Lady Diana Spencer into a princess. On September 6, 1997, London's streets were filled with crowds for the princess once more. But this time the people were not there to rejoice. Instead, they were there to say good-bye.

Diana's final journey was made in a coffin covered with royal flags and flowers and

Diana's body makes its final journey into Westminster Abbey. The flowers and card at the front are from Prince Harry.

carried through the streets on a horse-drawn carriage. One of the floral arrangements was a white wreath with a card that read "Mummy" in 12-year-old Harry's childlike handwriting. The procession began at Kensington Palace and wound its way through the streets to Westminster Abbey. Prince Charles, his father, Prince Phillip, Princes William and Harry, and Diana's brother, Earl Spencer, marched solemnly behind the carriage. More than 2.5 billion people watched the funeral procession on television, as well as the service that followed at Westminster Abbey. It was the largest television event in history, attracting more viewers than even Charles and Diana's wedding.

> ## Westminster Abbey
>
> Located in London, Westminster Abbey is the most famous church in Great Britain. King Edward the Confessor began the church in 1050, and construction continued in stages until the abbey was finally completed eight hundred years later. British kings and queen have been crowned at the abbey since William the Conqueror in 1066, and many of the nation's monarchs are buried there. Westminster Abbey also holds the tombs of many of Great Britain's writers, scientists, and other notable citizens.

The congregation inside Westminster Abbey was a mixture of heads of state, celebrities, and many representatives of the charities Diana had given so much of her time to. Rock star Elton John performed his song "Candle in the Wind," with words specially written to honor Diana. The performance moved many in the church, including Prince Harry, to tears.

Diana's brother gave her eulogy. Earl Spencer's fiery speech

Commemorative plaques line the Princess Diana Memorial Walk in London.

not only paid tribute to "the unique, the complex, the extraordinary, and irreplaceable Diana" but attacked the media for their "permanent quest to bring her down." Finally, Spencer turned on the royal family itself, promising Diana that the Spencer family would do everything it could to "continue the imaginative way in which you were steering these two exceptional young men [William and Harry], so that their souls are not simply immersed by duty and tradition but can sing openly as you planned." The crowds outside burst into thunderous applause while the royal family sat in stony silence.

After the funeral, Diana's coffin was loaded into a hearse and driven to the Spencer family's estate at Althorp. There, in a private service attended only by the Spencer family, Diana was buried on an island in the middle of the lake. Finally, the "Queen of Hearts" was at peace.

Diana continued to monopolize news headlines after her death. As she had been in life, Diana was the focus of many books, magazines, television programs, and other media tributes. People rushed to collect Diana memorabilia, such as dolls and plates imprinted with the princess's picture.

Londoners also worked to create physical tributes to their beloved princess. In June 2000, the Princess Diana Memorial Walk was completed in Kensington Gardens. The seven-mile

(11.3-kilometer) walkway runs through London's parks and passes important places in Diana's life, such as Kensington Palace and Buckingham Palace. The walkway also includes a large playground which is accessible to children with disabilities and reflects Diana's love of children.

For many years, organizers struggled to erect a permanent memorial to Diana in London. Finally, in July 2004, Queen Elizabeth officially unveiled the Princess Diana Memorial Fountain in Hyde Park. The fountain features two rings of flowing water encircling a green park. Prince Charles, William and Harry, and Earl Spencer also attended the ceremony, at which Queen Elizabeth called Diana a "remarkable human being" and spoke of "the extraordinary effect Diana had on those around her" and her ability "not only to touch people's lives but to change them."

As the years passed, life returned to normal for the people Diana left behind. William and Harry graduated from Eton, a prestigious school in London. William went on to

Diana's sons have grown into handsome young men and are still the focus of the world's attention.

study art history at St. Andrews University in Scotland, where he graduated in 2005. After graduating from Eton, Prince Harry entered Sandhurst Military Academy in 2005 to train for a military career.

Life went on for Prince Charles as well. The media's and public's dislike toward Camilla Parker Bowles gradually subsided, and the two eventually married in April 2005.

Diana's legacy lives on today through humanitarian works. Immediately after her death, people began donating money in her memory. The donations totaled more than $30 million, and the Diana, Princess of Wales Memorial Fund was started in September 1997 to distribute the money. The Fund concentrates on supporting charities that the princess had connections with during her life, including those for landmine victims, AIDS victims, and homeless children.

Diana's legacy also lives on in her children. After Diana's funeral, the royal family cut off contact with Earl Spencer for many years, and Diana's brother never got to fulfill his promise to influence his nephews' lives. Although William and Harry were raised completely in the royal tradition, they have emerged as well-rounded, mature, and caring young men who have a close relationship with their father while still honoring their mother.

The princes are determined to continue the charitable work that was so important to Princess Diana, and both William and Harry have volunteered for charities and traveled abroad to help the less fortunate. British students traditionally take a "gap year" before they start college. During this year, students work, travel, or volunteer for charitable causes. As part of his gap year, Prince Harry spent eight weeks in Lesotho, Africa, working with children orphaned by AIDS. While in Lesotho, he filmed a documentary, during which he spoke candidly for the first time about his mother and her influence on his life. "I believe I've got a lot of my mother in me," he said, "and I think she'd want us to do this, me and my brother. I don't want to take over from her because I never will. I don't think anyone can, but I want to try to carry it on to make her proud."

Prince Harry spent eight weeks in Africa working with AIDS orphans. He and his brother are determined to carry on their mother's humanitarian efforts.

Princess Diana once said, "Being constantly in the public eye gives me a special responsibility." Diana took that responsibility seriously and made a difference in the world, in spite of scandals, personal troubles, and a life lived largely in the glare of the media. Diana became much more than the "people's princess." She became a powerful public figure and humanitarian who made a real difference in the world. Hers is one of the most fascinating lives of the 20th century.

Events in the Life of Princess Diana

1979
Diana moves to London and begins working at the Young England Kindergarten.

June 21, 1982
The couple's first son, Prince William, is born.

July 1, 1961
Diana Frances Spencer is born.

June 9, 1975
Diana's father becomes the eighth Earl Spencer, and Diana becomes Lady Diana Spencer.

February 6, 1981
Charles asks Diana to marry him.

September 15, 1984
The couple's second son, Prince Harry, is born.

July 1980
Diana talks to Prince Charles at length for the first time.

July 29, 1981
Diana and Charles are married at St. Paul's Cathedral.

March 1983
Diana, Charles, and William tour Australia and New Zealand.

1969
Diana's parents divorce, and her father wins custody of the children.

1992
Andrew Morton's book, *Diana: Her True Story*, is published.

June 25, 1997
Many of Diana's dresses are auctioned at Christie's in New York, raising $3.26 million for charity.

August 31, 1997
Diana and Dodi Fayed are killed in a car crash inside the Alma Tunnel in Paris.

November 20, 1995
Diana appears in a candid interview on the British TV show *Panorama*.

December 9, 1992
Diana and Prince Charles officially separate.

July 11, 1997
Diana arrives on the *Jonikal* for a vacation with Dodi Fayed.

1987
Diana visits the first British hospital ward for AIDS patients and changes the perception of the disease when she shakes hands with a patient.

August 28, 1996
Charles and Diana's divorce becomes official.

September 6, 1997
Diana's funeral is held in Westminster Abbey, and she is buried at Althorp, the Spencer family estate.

Bibliography

BOOKS

Andersen, Christopher. *The Day Diana Died.* New York: William Morrow and Company, Inc., 1998.

Burrell, Paul. *A Royal Duty.* New York: G.P. Putnam's Sons, 2003.

Clayton, Tim and Phil Craig. *Diana: Story of a Princess.* New York: Pocket Books, 2001.

Graham, Tim. *Dressing Diana.* New York: Welcome Rain, 1998.

Jephson, P.D. *Shadows of a Princess: Diana, Princess of Wales: An Intimate Account by Her Private Secretary.* New York: HarperCollins, 2000.

Licata, Renora. *Princess Diana: Royal Ambassador.* Woodbridge, Connecticut: Blackbirch Press, 1993.

Martin, Ralph G. *Charles and Diana.* New York: Putnam, 1985.

Morton, Andrew. *Diana: Her True Story.* New York: Simon and Schuster, 1997.

Vickers, Hugo. *Debrett's Book of the Royal Wedding.* New York: Viking Press, 1981.

VIDEO

Diana, A Celebration. BBC Video/CBS Fox Video, 1997.

CD-ROM

Microsoft Encarta 2000.

Sources Cited

pp.10–11:	"I always had this thing inside me..." *Diana: Her True Story,* p. 25.
pp.12–13:	"Diana knew she was a...swimmer..." *Diana: Story of a Princess,* p. 11.
pp.16–17:	"a very jolly and amusing..." *Diana: Her True Story,* p. 95.
pp.18–19:	"It was nice being in a flat with the girls..." *Diana: Her True Story,* p.30.
pp.20–21:	"She was very good..." *Diana: Story of a Princess,* p. 27.
pp.28–29:	"I knew your legs were good..." *Diana: Story of a Princess,* p. 42.
pp.28-29:	"We urged it along..." *Diana: Story of a Princess,* p. 52.
pp.30–31:	"Yes, Whatever love means" *Diana: Her True Story,* p. 34.
pp.34–35:	"Please don't call me that..." *The Day Diana Died,* p. 39.
pp.34–35:	"Your face is on the tea-towels..." *Diana: Her True Story,* p. 124.
pp.46–47:	"At William's christening..." *Diana: Her True Story,* p. 46.

pp.50–51: "Then suddenly as Harry was born…" *Diana: Her True Story*, p. 51.

pp.52–53: "the one we all want to look like…" *Princess Diana: Royal Ambassador*, p. 45.

pp.58–59: "made a tremendous impact…" *Diana: Story of a Princess*, p. 159.

pp.60–61: "The questions she asked…" *Diana: Story of a Princess*, pp. 182-183, 185.

pp.70–71: "I was at the end of my tether…" *The Day Diana Died*, p. 46.

pp.76–77: "I cried all the way out…" *Diana: Her True Story*, p. 232.

pp.76–77: "I appoint my mother and my brother…" *The Day Diana Died*, p. 50.

pp.78–79: "I pay attention to people…" *The Day Diana Died*, p. 50.

pp.82–83: "I hope you can find it in your hearts…" *Diana: Story of a Princess*, p. 260.

pp.88–89: "hidden upstairs with the governess…" *Diana: Her True Story*, p. 251.

pp.90–91: "There were three of us in this marriage…" *Diana: Her True Story*, p. 245.

pp.94–95: "I don't mind what you're called…" *The Day Diana Died*, p. 57.

pp.96–97: "I can't think of anybody…" *Diana: Story of a Princess*, p. 320.

pp.110–111: "Photographers were swarming all over …" *The Day Diana Died*, p. 203.

pp.110–111: "The camera flashes were going off…" *The Day Diana Died*, p. 204.

pp.112–113: "This is going to produce…" *The Day Diana Died*, p. 223.

pp.114–115: "The monarchy must bow its head…" *The Day Diana Died*, p. 255.

pp. 116–117: "the unique, the complex…" *Diana: Her True Story*, p. 281.

pp.118–119: "a remarkable…" BBC News, http://news.bbc.co.uk/1/hi/uk/3866863.stm.

pp.120–121: "I believe…" BBC News, http://news.bbc.co.uk/1/hi/uk/3664654.stm.

pp.120–121: "Being constantly in the public eye…" The Diana, Princess of Wales Memorial Fund, http://www.theworkcontinues.org/aboutus/inherownwords.asp.

For Further Study

Princess Diana's life has been heavily covered by the media. Search the BBC News Web site at http://news.bbc.co.uk for many stories about her.

Since Diana's death, the Diana, Princess of Wales Memorial Fund has been raising and donating money to worthy causes. Find out about their mission at www.theworkcontinues.org.

The British monarchy is a treasure trove of history, culture, and tradition. Learn more about it at the official Web site of the British monarchy, www.royal.gov.uk.

The city of London has created several memorials to Princess Diana. See photos and find out about some of these tributes at http://infoplease.com/spot/diana1.html.

Index

Acknowledgments

This book is dedicated to Jim, my Prince Charming, and our three Little Princesses, Christina, Leanne, and Grace.

Picture Credits

The photographs in this book are used with permission and through the courtesy of (t=top; b=bottom; l=left; r=right): Associated Press. AP:pp.6-7, 30, 79; p.53 Tim Graham; Corbis:pp.8, 44-45 Hulton Deutsch;pp.18-19 Touhig Sion;p.22 Sygma/Beirne Brendon; pp.24-25 Patrick Ward; pp.26-27 Gideon Mendel; pp.32-33 Free Agents Limited;p.33r Murat Taner/Zefa; p.34 Quadrillon; pp.5-6, 31, 38-39, 41, 42, 48-49, 54-55, 59, 60, 73, 76-77, 78, 83, 92, 94, 96,102, 103, 110, 122tc, 123(bl-br) Tim Graham; p.43 Michael Boys; p.69 Reuters; pp.70,123tl Sygma/Polak; p.84, 100-101, 105 Sygma ; pp.88-89 Stan Roberts/Collier Photos; p.90 Sygma/B.B.C. Panorama; p.95 Sygma/Murray Andrew; p.107 Sygma/Pasquini Cedric; p.114 Liba Taylor;p.116 Sygma/Austral;p.119 Toby Melville; p.121 Kieran Doherty; Getty Images: pp.11,12-13, 17, 28-29, 36-37, 46-47, 52, 72, 122(tl-tr-bl-br);124-125,126-127; pp.14, 58, 62-63 Tim Graham; Rex Features,Ltd.:pp.19tr, 20-21, 23, 35, 50, 56-57, 64, 67, 68, 74-75, 80, 85, 86-87, 91, 98-99, 108, 109, 112-113, 115, 118, 123tr. Border Photos, from left to right: Getty Images,Getty Images,Corbis/Tim Graham,Getty Images, Getty Images/Tim Graham, Corbis/ Quadrillion,Corbis/Quadrillion,Getty Images,Corbis/Tim Graham,Corbis/Hulton Deutsch Collection,Getty Images,Corbis/Tim Graham,Getty Images,Corbis/Reuters,Corbis/Reuters.

About the Author

Joanne Mattern has always loved working with books. She has worked in libraries off and on since the age of 14. After obtaining a degree in English from Hartwick College in Oneonta, New York, Mattern worked as an editor at Morrow Junior Books and Troll Communications for 10 years. Her first children's book, a retelling of *The Adventures of Tom Sawyer*, was published by Troll Communications in 1990, and she's been writing ever since! So far, she has published more than 150 books for young readers. Mattern specializes in nonfiction and especially loves writing about animals, sports, interesting people, and important historical events. She lives with her husband, James, three daughters, Christina, Leanne, and Grace, and several cats and other pets in the beautiful Hudson Valley of New York state.

Other DK Biographies you may enjoy:

DK Biography: *Albert Einstein*
by Frieda Wishinsky
ISBN 0-7566-1247-0 paperback
ISBN 0-7566-1248-9 hardcover

DK Biography: *Anne Frank*
by Kem Knapp Sawyer
ISBN 0-7566-0341-2 paperback
ISBN 0-7566-0490-7 hardcover

DK Biography: *Helen Keller*
by Leslie Garrett
ISBN 0-7566-0339-0 paperback
ISBN 0-7566-0488-5 hardcover

DK Biography: *John F. Kennedy*
by Howard S. Kaplan
ISBN 0-7566-0340-4 paperback
ISBN 0-7566-0489-3 hardcover

DK Biography: *Martin Luther King, Jr.*
by Amy Pastan
ISBN 0-7566-0342-0 paperback
ISBN 0-7566-0491-5 hardcover

DK Biography: *Abraham Lincoln*
by Tanya Lee Stone
ISBN 0-7566-0341-2 paperback
ISBN 0-7566-0490-7 hardcover

DK Biography: *George Washington*
by Lenny Hort
ISBN 0-7566-0835-X paperback
ISBN 0-7566-0832-5 hardcover

DK Biography: *Eleanor Roosevelt*
by Kem Knapp Sawyer
ISBN 0-7566-1496-1 paperback
ISBN 0-7566-1495-3 hardcover

Look what the critics are saying about DK Biography!

"…highly readable, worthwhile overviews for young people…"—*Booklist*

"This new series from the inimitable DK Publishing brings together the usual brilliant photography with a historian's approach to biography subjects."
—*Ingram Library Services*